DISCARD

The Bombing of Hiroshima

The Bombing of Hiroshima

John Ziff

CHELSEA HOUSE PUBLISHERS
Philadelphia

Frontispiece: The hands of Kengo Nikawa's pocket watch froze at the exact moment the atomic bomb struck Hiroshima, August 6, 1945.

CHELSEA HOUSE PUBLISHERS

Editor in Chief Sally Cheney
Associate Editor in Chief Kim Shinners
Production Manager Pamela Loos
Art Director Sara Davis
Director of Photography Judy L. Hasday
Senior Production Editor J. Christopher Higgins

Staff for THE BOMBING OF HIROSHIMA

Senior Editor James D. Gallagher, LeeAnne Gelletly
Associate Art Director/Designer Takeshi Takahashi
Picture Researcher Patricia Burns
Cover Designer Takeshi Takahashi

First Printing

1 3 5 7 9 8 6 4 2

The Chelsea House World Wide Web address is
http://www.chelseahouse.com

Library of Congress Cataloging-in-Publication Data

Ziff, John.
The bombing of Hiroshima / John Ziff.
    p. cm. — (Great disasters, reforms and ramifications)

ISBN 0-7910-5786-0 (alk. paper)

1. Hiroshima-shi (Japan)—History—Bombardment, 1945. I. Series.

D767.25.H6 Z54 2001
940.54'25—dc21

00-048548

Contents

GREAT DISASTERS
REFORMS and RAMIFICATIONS

Jill McCaffrey
National Chairman
Armed Forces Emergency Services
American Red Cross

Introduction

Disasters have always been a source of fascination and awe. Tales of a great flood that nearly wipes out all life are among humanity's oldest recorded stories, dating at least from the second millennium B.C., and they appear in cultures from the Middle East to the Arctic Circle to the southernmost tip of South America and the islands of Polynesia. Typically gods are at the center of these ancient disaster tales—which is perhaps not too surprising, given the fact that the tales originated during a time when human beings were at the mercy of natural forces they did not understand.

To a great extent, we still are at the mercy of nature, as anyone who reads the newspapers or watches nightly news broadcasts can attest.

Hurricanes, earthquakes, tornados, wildfires, and floods continue to exact a heavy toll in suffering and death, despite our considerable knowledge of the workings of the physical world. If science has offered only limited protection from the consequences of natural disasters, it has in no way diminished our fascination with them. Perhaps that's because the scale and power of natural disasters force us as individuals to confront our relatively insignificant place in the physical world and remind us of the fragility and transience of our lives. Perhaps it's because we can imagine ourselves in the midst of dire circumstances and wonder how we would respond. Perhaps it's because disasters seem to bring out the best and worst instincts of humanity: altruism and selfishness, courage and cowardice, generosity and greed.

As one of the national chairmen of the American Red Cross, a humanitarian organization that provides relief for victims of disasters, I have had the privilege of seeing some of humanity's best instincts. I have witnessed communities pulling together in the face of trauma; I have seen thousands of people answer the call to help total strangers in their time of need.

Of course, helping victims after a tragedy is not the only way, or even the best way, to deal with disaster. In many cases planning and preparation can minimize damage and loss of life—or even avoid a disaster entirely. For, as history repeatedly shows, many disasters are caused not by nature but by human folly, shortsightedness, and unethical conduct. For example, when a land developer wanted to create a lake for his exclusive resort club in Pennsylvania's Allegheny Mountains in 1880, he ignored expert warnings and cut corners in reconstructing an earthen dam. On May 31, 1889, the dam gave way, unleashing 20 million tons of water on the towns below. The Johnstown Flood, the deadliest in American history, claimed more than 2,200 lives. Greed and negligence would figure prominently in the Triangle Shirtwaist Company fire in 1911. Deplorable conditions in the garment sweatshop, along with a failure to give any thought to the safety of workers, led to the tragic deaths of 146 persons. Technology outstripped wisdom only a year later, when the designers of the luxury liner *Titanic* smugly declared their state-of-the-art ship "unsinkable," seeing no need to provide lifeboat capacity for everyone onboard. On the night of April 14, 1912, more than 1,500 passengers and crew paid for this hubris with their lives after the ship collided with an iceberg and sank. But human catastrophes aren't always the unforeseen consequences of carelessness or folly. In the 1940s the leaders of Nazi Germany purposefully and systematically set out to exterminate all Jews, along with Gypsies, homosexuals, the mentally ill, and other so-called undesirables. More recently terrorists have targeted random members of society, blowing up airplanes and buildings in an effort to advance their political agendas.

The books in the GREAT DISASTERS: REFORMS AND RAMIFICATIONS series examine these and other famous disasters, natural and human made. They explain the causes of the disasters, describe in detail how events unfolded, and paint vivid portraits of the people caught up in dangerous circumstances. But these books are more than just accounts of what happened to whom and why. For they place the disasters in historical perspective, showing how people's attitudes and actions changed and detailing the steps society took in the wake of each calamity. And in the end, the most important lesson we can learn from any disaster—as well as the most fitting tribute to those who suffered and died—is how to avoid a repeat in the future.

A new age dawns in the remote New Mexico desert near Alamogordo, July 16, 1945. Never again would humanity be safe from the threat of annihilation.

Destroyer of Worlds

In the predawn hours of July 16, 1945, a bizarre scene unfolded in the New Mexico desert near Alamogordo. On a hilltop at the edge of a remote area known as the Jornada del Muerto—Spanish for Journey of Death—a group of men stood in the pitch-blackness of the night and slathered their skin with suntan lotion. Minutes later the men donned sunglasses, some also pressing extra-dark welder's shields to their faces. It was as though they feared sunburn from the stars or expected moonlight to suddenly turn blinding. It was as though they believed the natural world as humanity had experienced it since the dawn of civilization was about to change.

Similar thoughts seemed to be occurring to another group of men about 30 miles to the southeast. In a shallow trench these men lay shoulder to shoulder, like soldiers on the front line awaiting an attack. Yet they carried no weapons. Like the men on the distant hilltop, however, they were outfitted with sunglasses and welder's shields in the inky darkness.

Between the group on the hilltop and the group in the trench lay three earthen dugouts, with stout oak beams supporting their concrete-slab roofs. On a map, an arc connecting these three shelters would form a parenthesis tilted slightly toward the rounded side. What that parenthesis seemed to enclose was a steel tower 10,000 yards— about 5.7 miles—away from each of the three shelters, which stood at points roughly north, west, and south of the 100-foot-high structure. The north and west shelters contained a battery of equipment: searchlights, recording instruments, high-speed cameras. If—as the peculiar behavior of the people in the Jornada del Muerto suggested—something extraordinary was going to happen on this night, then that event would be well documented by the equipment in the north and west shelters. The south shelter, by contrast, housed equipment that seemed designed not to record but to initiate—specifically, a console cluttered with various lights, electrical gauges, a timing mechanism, and a switch.

Hours before the men on the hilltop and in the trench donned their sunglasses, a small crowd had gathered in the south shelter. As night marched inexorably toward dawn, this group was afflicted by a feeling of growing, and almost unbearable, tension. No one felt the tension more keenly than a pair of men who in physical appearance vaguely resembled the comic team of Stan Laurel and Oliver Hardy: one thin and clean-cut, the other fat and mustachioed. Those who knew these men might have recalled a more literary pair: the idealistic dreamer Don Quixote and his pragmatic sidekick Sancho Panza, creations of the Spanish writer Miguel de Cervantes.

Like that fictional duo, the two men in the earthen shelter could hardly have been more different in personality and temperament.

Standing six feet tall and weighing less than 120 pounds, the thin one, J. Robert Oppenheimer, was a true Renaissance man. A former child prodigy, Oppie—as his colleagues sometimes called him—had delivered his first scientific paper at the tender age of 11. He spoke French and German fluently, read the works of Plato in classical Greek, and had taught himself Sanskrit, an ancient literary language of India, just so he could read the philosophical poem *Bhagavad-Gita* in its original form. That poem, a meditation on the meaning of life and the nature of reality, is one of the Hindu religion's sacred texts. In it the god Krishna counsels Arjuna, a prince, on the eve of a battle Arjuna is reluctant to join because he doesn't want to kill his cousins. Urging Arjuna to do his duty as

Aerial view of one of the observation shelters located 5.7 miles from the test site.

a warrior, Krishna reveals that death isn't the end of the true self, for the material world that people see and hear and feel is really *maya,* or illusion.

Oppenheimer's interest in the nature of reality wasn't merely philosophical. He also explored an unseen realm few people could ever understand through his chosen field: theoretical physics. Educated at Harvard University, where he graduated summa cum laude in just three years, he had gone to Europe to pursue further studies at the world's leading centers of physics: the Cavendish Laboratory in England, the University of Leyden in the Netherlands, the University of Göttingen in Germany. Upon returning to the United States, he had received appointments to the California Institute of Technology and the University of California at Berkeley, whose physics department he helped build into one of the finest in the country.

Now, at age 41, Oppenheimer was in his third year at the head of an extraordinary collection of scientists, mathematicians, and engineers, including a large number of past and future Nobel Prize winners. Not surprisingly, the group contained some eccentrics—and a healthy share of substantial egos. But with charismatic leadership, formidable administrative skills, and a subtle mind capable of quickly grasping implications, Oppenheimer was able to keep this difficult group from disintegrating through long months of an exceedingly complex and often frustrating project. Had he not earned the trust, respect—even admiration—of his distinguished colleagues, it's likely that on this July night the Jornada del Muerto would have belonged solely to its usual denizens: snakes, jackrabbits, and scorpions.

It's also likely that the desert would have been devoid of human activity without Oppenheimer's obese counterpart in the south shelter. Yet words like *trust, respect,* and *admiration* weren't often heard when colleagues spoke of General Leslie R. Groves. Groves—whose weight remained a closely guarded secret, though best estimates put it at about 300 pounds—was a bully who routinely browbeat and publicly humiliated subordinates. Once, in the middle of an important meeting, he stripped off his tunic and thrust it at a top deputy, whom he loudly ordered to have the garment dry-cleaned. Aides were expected to keep his office safe stocked with the one-pound boxes of chocolates he devoured. Though his reputation depended on the work of the theoretical scientists, Groves seemed to go out of his way to antagonize them. He didn't understand their world of particles and forces, but he was nevertheless convinced they were undisciplined crackpots—and didn't hesitate to say so.

Physicist J. Robert Oppenheimer and General Leslie R. Groves, the scientific and military leaders of the atomic bomb project, examine the remains of the 100-foot steel tower that housed the test bomb. Everything was vaporized except the reinforcing rods at the tower's base.

Despite his grating personality, however, the general did have an undeniable gift for breaking through bureaucratic and logistical barriers to get a job done. Trained as an engineer, he had, three years earlier, been in charge of all U.S. military construction, including the Pentagon Building in Washington, D.C. But by 1942, the career military man who had graduated fourth in his class from the United States Military Academy at West Point longed to command tanks and infantry divisions, not bulldozers and architects and construction workers. To his dismay, however, the army had once again tapped him for a stateside project—though it softened the blow by promoting him from colonel to brigadier general.

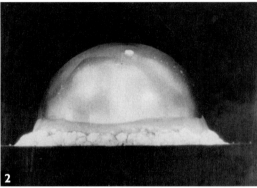

Now, on this July night three years later, the moment of truth had arrived for Groves, and for his colleague Oppenheimer. America had invested $2 billion in the project that this oddest of odd couples led, and the question of whether that money had been completely wasted was about to be answered.

Around 2 A.M., in the midst of lightning, thunder, and a torrential rain driven by 30-mile-per-hour winds, Groves and Oppenheimer met with their chief meteorologist, Jack Hubbard. "What the hell is wrong with the weather?" Groves growled. Hubbard insisted that the weather would break between 5 and 6 o'clock. "You'd better be right on this," the general warned, "or I will hang you."

Time proved the meteorologist correct, and under clearing skies Groves departed the south shelter a little

after 5 o'clock. With characteristic self-regard, he considered himself and Oppenheimer *the* indispensable members of the project, and he didn't want a catastrophe to claim both of their lives simultaneously. So he drove his Jeep five miles south to the site known as Base Camp, where the men were lying shoulder to shoulder in the trench.

As Groves took up position in that trench, Oppenheimer, his legs having suddenly turned to jelly, hugged a post in the south shelter for support. He stared straight ahead, barely breathing. Was he haunted by the prospect of failure—or by a premonition that success might have consequences that were even more dire?

A gong sounded. Moments later, at 15 seconds before 5:30 A.M., night instantly gave way to a daylight infinitely brighter than the noontime sun, a light so brilliant and

An army motion-picture camera captured images of the July 16 test. The sequence on these pages represents less than half a second. Note the bright flash of light in the first frame and the rapid expansion of the fireball.

piercing that, a witness recalled, "it bored its way right through you. It was a vision which was seen with more than the eye." Indeed, a blind woman was among the dozens of residents within a 300-mile radius who flooded sheriff's departments and newspapers with reports of an otherworldly flash of light.

The false day produced by that flash of light lasted only about two seconds, but the strange spectacle wasn't over. From the point designated Zero—the site of the 100-foot-tall steel tower—a fiery orb appeared low to the horizon like the rising sun. The sphere expanded rapidly, but soon its lower third was obscured by a ring of dust and smoke. The ring became a cloud and blew up and out like an open umbrella, almost completely hiding the ball of fire. But then the fireball slowly began ascending into the sky, seemingly pushed upward on the cloud of dust and smoke, which now appeared to be growing out of the ground like the stem of a giant, twisting plant. The rising fireball darkened to a deep, glowing purple. High above it, the clouds that remained from the storm that had earlier caused General Groves so much consternation were pierced by an expanding circular hole.

On the ground, more than 10 miles away from Zero at Base Camp, observers watching all this from the trench suddenly felt a wave of heat overwhelm the chill of the desert night, as though an oven door had been opened. And throughout the Jornada del Muerto a rumbling sound like thunder echoed for what seemed an eternity.

"Most experiences in life can be comprehended by prior experiences," observed physicist Norris Bradbury, a witness to the spectacle. But this "did not fit into any pre-conceptions possessed by anybody."

The laws of nature had not changed, but humanity's relationship to the physical world had been profoundly— and permanently—altered. Observed I. I. Rabi, a physicist and key aide to Oppenheimer, "A new thing had just been born; a new control; a new understanding of man, which man had acquired over nature."

Oppenheimer's scientists had successfully performed the largest physics experiment in history. They had unlocked the enormous energy of the strong nuclear force—the force that binds together the nuclei of atoms. As the realization of their achievement sank in, scientists broke into spontaneous celebrations. William L. Laurence, a *New York Times* correspondent, noted those around him "shaking hands, slapping each other on the back, laughing like happy children"—even dancing "like primitive man . . . at one of his fire festivals at the coming of spring."

But not everyone was so jubilant. "At first I was thrilled," Rabi recalled. "Then, a few minutes afterward, I had gooseflesh all over me when I realized what this meant for the future of humanity."

Oppenheimer's thoughts turned to the *Bhagavad-Gita:*

We waited until the blast had passed, walked out of the shelter and then it was extremely solemn. We knew the world would not be the same. A few people laughed, a few people cried. Most people were silent. I remembered the line from the Hindu scripture, the *Bhagavad-Gita*: [Krishna] is trying to persuade the Prince that he should do his duty and to impress him he takes on his multi-armed form and says, "Now I am become Death, the destroyer of worlds." I suppose we all thought that, one way or another.

The military men present saw things from a different perspective. "The war is over," General Thomas Farrell told his boss, General Groves.

"Yes," Groves replied, "after we drop two bombs on Japan."

Prelude to the Pacific War

German soldiers roll through a town in Belgium, May 1940. The first months of World War II saw a series of relatively easy victories for Germany and grave setbacks for Europe's democracies.

2

The war General Groves proposed to end by dropping two bombs on Japan, World War II, had already been the most savage and destructive conflict in human history. Nearly six years of fighting on land, at sea, and in the air had claimed the lives of up to 20 million servicemen from the two dozen nations involved in the conflict. As many as 25 million civilians had also perished.

The fighting began on September 1, 1939, when Nazi Germany launched a blitzkrieg, or "lightning war," against Poland, its neighbor to the east. For six years Nazi dictator Adolf Hitler had been inching his country toward this point. In 1933 Hitler began rearming Germany, in violation of the Treaty of Versailles, which had ended the First World War. In 1935 he instituted universal military service, and the following year he ordered troops into the demilitarized Rhineland. In 1938 he forced the German-speaking nation of Austria to unite with his Nazi Third Reich. That same year, at the Munich Conference, attended by Germany, France, and England, he demanded—and received—the Sudetenland region of Czechoslovakia under the pretext that the ethnic German minority there was being persecuted. This, Hitler promised, would be Germany's last territorial demand. It wasn't. In March 1939 German troops occupied Czechoslovakia.

Throughout this time, Europe's most powerful democracies, France and Great Britain, had watched idly as Hitler became ever bolder. But with a growing sense that the Nazi dictator's territorial ambitions knew no bounds, in spring 1939 the two nations drew a line in the sand: they would oppose any Nazi aggression in Poland. So on September 3, 1939, two days after German tank, infantry, and air units had streamed across the border and set the Polish countryside ablaze, France and Great Britain declared war on Germany.

Unfortunately, it was already too late to save Poland, which fell to the Nazis within two weeks. Hitler and Joseph Stalin—the Soviet Union's Communist dictator, who had earlier signed a secret nonaggression pact with his Nazi counterpart—then proceeded to divide up the conquered nation.

During the winter of 1939–40, the fighting in Europe was mostly confined to naval warfare. But then, in early April 1940, the Germans once again took the initiative on the ground. Using a vanguard of quick-moving mechanized units supported by intense air power—the blitzkrieg formula that had proved so successful in Poland—the Nazis won a string of rapid victories. To the north, the Germans subdued Denmark within days of their April 9 invasion. The conquest of Norway, on the

Scandinavian Peninsula, took only slightly longer, despite the efforts of British and French soldiers to mute the onslaught. Next, Hitler's forces turned west. On May 10, Nazi units swept into the Low Countries—the Netherlands, Belgium, and Luxembourg. Luxembourg offered no resistance; the Netherlands fell within a week, Belgium within two.

On May 16 Hitler's armies poured into France through the Ardennes region of Belgium. A wooded area, the Ardennes wasn't the easiest terrain from which to launch an attack. But the extra effort paid off for the Germans: not only were they able to avoid the Maginot Line, a string of defensive fortifications France had constructed along its border with Germany, but they also surprised the French army and the British Expeditionary Force (BEF), which were concentrated farther north in anticipation of an attack through the plains of Belgium. The Germans quickly pushed the Allies back, and only a massive evacuation from the beaches of Dunkirk saved the BEF and their French comrades—some 338,000 strong—from capture or annihilation.

The fall of France was by this time a foregone conclusion. Seeking an easy victory and a share of the spoils, the Italian Fascist dictator Benito Mussolini declared war

Nazi dictator Adolf Hitler (front row, second from right) and his commanders in Paris, June 25, 1940. The fall of France left Great Britain alone against the German war machine. Although public sentiment in America lay with the embattled British, an official policy of neutrality prevailed.

The dome of St. Paul's Cathedral in London rises above smoke from fires ignited by a German air raid. During the summer of 1940, Germany's air force, the Luftwaffe, incessantly bombed England.

on England and France on June 10. On June 14 the German army marched into Paris, and on the 22nd Hitler forced France to sign a humiliating armistice.

Thus, as the summer of 1940 began, Great Britain stood alone against the Nazi war machine. Protected from invasion only by the narrow waters of the English Channel, England's position seemed precarious indeed.

From across a much wider body of water, Franklin Delano Roosevelt watched these developments with great concern. The three-term American president considered Hitler's Nazis a grave, if not an immediate, threat to the United States. Should Great Britain fall, what would prevent Germany from seeking additional conquests across the Atlantic? With western Europe under its heel, the Third Reich could match America's industrial output, and, facing no other enemies on the battlefield, it could direct its full military might against the United States. Plus, it would have the luxury of initiating the fight when it was ready. If the United States was going to confront Germany, Roosevelt knew, it would be far better to do so alongside a credible ally like Great Britain. Unfortunately, there was no guarantee the British would be able to hold off the Nazis for any length of time.

While he may have wished that his nation could join the fight sooner rather than later, the president had neither the political justification nor the public consensus to commit American troops to the war. The United States had not been attacked, and public opinion favored staying out of what was widely seen as a strictly European problem.

Isolationism—the idea that the country was better off avoiding alliances and staying out of international affairs as much as possible—had long been embraced by the American people and their elected officials. After World War I, Congress had blocked U.S. participation in the League of Nations, an international organization designed to help resolve conflicts peacefully. Later, Congress had passed neutrality laws forbidding the sale of military supplies to any nation fighting a war.

The Roosevelt administration's hands were to a great extent tied. But that's not to say the president didn't find a way to aid Great Britain. Revised neutrality legislation passed in 1939 permitted the United States to sell military equipment to all nations. However, no American ships or citizens could transport that equipment; rather, the purchasing nation had to pick it up in the United States and had to pay in cash. Theoretically, the law favored no one nation because any nation could buy military supplies in this manner. In practice, however, Great Britain was the sole beneficiary because it controlled the seas. In March 1941 the passage of the Lend-Lease Act further extended American economic aid to the embattled English. The act gave the president authority to ship war supplies to any nation whose defense he deemed vital to America's security.

By that time Great Britain had staved off a planned Nazi invasion by defeating the Luftwaffe, Germany's air force, in a two-month-long battle over the skies of England. Lacking superiority in the air, Germany couldn't undertake a crossing of the English Channel, because its troop transport ships would be vulnerable to Royal Air Force planes. Still, Britain's long-range military prospects were far from rosy. Both Winston Churchill, England's prime minister, and President Roosevelt looked for a way to pull the United States into the fight against Germany.

By the end of 1941 an event would occur that would galvanize the American people and give Roosevelt the justification he needed to lead his country into World War II. Surprisingly, that event would have nothing to do with Nazi Germany. In fact, it wouldn't even occur in Europe. Rather, America would be drawn into the war by actions taken half a world away, in the Pacific Ocean, by the empire of Japan.

Like Nazi Germany, Imperial Japan had fallen under the siren song of militarism and extreme nationalism beginning in the early 1930s. For decades Japanese leaders had sought to make their country the foremost economic, political, and military power in Asia. Unfortunately, nature had dealt the island nation a bad hand: Japan lacked the natural resources necessary to sustain a modern industrial economy. It was thus especially dependent on access to foreign markets. Trade with China, on the Asian mainland to the west, was particularly critical to Japan's economic development; the China trade was also highly prized by the United States and the European powers. In the 1920s Japan had joined the Western nations in pledging to respect the territorial integrity of its neighbor on the mainland and in agreeing to the Open Door policy, which guaranteed all nations the opportunity to trade in China. By the following decade, however, the military leaders who increasingly held sway in the Japanese government had embarked on a different course.

On September 18, 1931, officers in Japan's Kwantung Army exploded a bomb on the South Manchurian Railroad in China. Ironically, that railroad was Japanese operated, and the Kwantung Army had been stationed in the northeastern Chinese region of Manchuria for the express purpose of protecting it. Publicly blaming Chinese forces for the bombing, the Japanese proceeded to conquer all of Manchuria and set up a puppet state called Manchukuo. When the League of Nations condemned Japan's actions in the Manchurian Incident, Japan simply withdrew from the organization. As would soon be the case with Adolf Hitler in Europe, the international community took no meaningful steps to counter Japanese expansionism. Isolationist America simply protested Japan's aggression and refused to recognize Manchukuo. For Japan, the diplomatic flak was a small price to pay for the acquisition of the resource-rich land.

But Japan's designs on China weren't finished. On July 7, 1937, Japanese and Chinese soldiers fought a minor skirmish at the Marco Polo Bridge near Peking. Japan seized upon the incident as justification for conquering all of China.

Soldiers of Japan's Kwantung Army hurl grenades at Chinese troops in fighting near the Marco Polo Bridge, July 1937. The Japanese used the incident, a minor skirmish near Peking, to justify their drive to conquer all of China. The United States condemned Japan's aggression, and relations between the two nations deteriorated.

Japan's brutal tactics in the China campaign—including its use of aerial bombing against civilian populations, and a six-week-long orgy of rape and murder in the conquered city of Nanking—drew international outrage. President Roosevelt called for action to "quarantine the aggressors," and U.S.-Japanese relations entered a long downward spiral. Again, however, neither the United States nor the international community as a whole mustered a meaningful military response to the aggression. By 1939 Japan had subjugated eastern China, the richest and most populous region of the country.

Snuffing out all Chinese resistance would prove considerably more difficult, however. China is a large country, and much of its territory is extremely rugged. Instead of allowing themselves to be drawn into a decisive campaign along the plains of eastern China, which the far-stronger Japanese forces would surely win, the Chinese retreated into their country's interior, where geography would work to their advantage. In northern China, Communist guerrilla units checked the Japanese advance near the last great bend of the Yellow River, then harassed the Japanese invaders with continual hit-and-run attacks. Farther south, Chiang Kai-shek, the leader of the Nationalist forces and the man the United States recognized as China's legitimate ruler, retreated up the Yangtze River to Chungking. Protected by the Yangtze's massive gorges, the Nationalists could not be dislodged. Meanwhile, the United States funneled aid to Chiang's government. Japanese troops would, it seemed, be bogged down in China for a long time.

Still, by 1940 militarists in Japan saw new opportunities for advancing their dream of domination over Asia. France, Great Britain, and the Netherlands all had colonies in Southeast Asia or the Indonesian archipelago. With Nazi Germany wreaking havoc on them at home, the Europeans' grip on their colonies would surely be loosened, and Japan might be able to pluck these strategic lands from their colonial masters. As time went by, seizing the European colonies began to seem like less of a luxury and more of a necessity. This was because American economic sanctions were threatening to erode Japan's war-making potential.

In 1939, reacting to continued Japanese aggressions in China, the United States had announced that it would terminate its trade agreement with Japan. The following year, American economic sanctions began to bite hard, as restrictions were placed on the sale to Japan of scrap iron, aviation fuel, and war materiel. When Japanese troops occupied the French colony of Indochina in July 1941, the Roosevelt administration froze all Japanese financial

Chiang Kai-shek (left), leader of the Chinese Nationalists, meets with President Franklin Delano Roosevelt of the United States and Prime Minister Winston Churchill of Great Britain. U.S. support of Chiang's forces angered Imperial Japan.

assets in the United States and clamped an oil embargo on Japan.

As relations with the United States deteriorated, Japan attempted to shore up its diplomatic position with the rest of the world. In September 1940 Japan had signed the Tripartite Pact with Nazi Germany and Fascist Italy. The Axis powers, as the three allies were called, promised to aid one another militarily should any of them be attacked by another nation not yet involved in World War II. In April of the following year, Japan concluded a five-year neutrality treaty with its longtime rival in East Asia, the Soviet Union. For the duration of the treaty, the two nations pledged not to go to war with each other.

In time Japan would discover just how little such

pledges between rivals can be worth. Joseph Stalin, the Soviet Union's leader, learned the lesson a lot sooner. In June 1941 Adolf Hitler launched Operation Barbarossa, an invasion of Russia, despite his nonaggression pact with the USSR. With the Soviets struggling for their very survival against the Nazis, another barrier to Japanese expansion in East Asia had suddenly been removed.

Meanwhile, Japan's leaders were considering two distinct options for dealing with the United States. The first—advocated by moderates in the Japanese government such as the prime minister, Prince Fumimaro Konoe—involved a negotiated settlement with the Americans. Japan had earlier in the year dispatched a peace envoy, Ambassador Kichisaburo Nomura, to Washington. In talks with Cordell Hull, the U.S. secretary of state, Nomura sought the removal of American economic sanctions against his country. But from the outset Hull insisted that the sanctions would remain until Japan agreed to accept certain conditions, including a withdrawal from China. The negotiations dragged on for months with no discernible progress.

The second option Japan was considering involved a military solution, the Southern Operation. The goal of this operation, favored by Japanese nationalists, would be the seizure of the rich European colonies south of China. This would give Japan access to many of the resources it needed to feed its military machine: tin, rubber, lumber, rice, and, most important, oil. If Japan controlled all of French Indochina; the British colonies of Burma, Malaya, and the strategic port of Singapore; and the oil-rich Dutch East Indies, the effects of America's trade embargo would be negated. Plus, aid that flowed up the Malay Peninsula to Chiang Kai-shek's Chinese Nationalists could be choked off, offering the possibility of a definitive victory in China.

Secretary of State Cordell Hull is flanked by Kichisaburo Nomura, Japan's ambassador to the United States, and Saburo Kurusu, a special envoy, during negotiations in Washington, D.C., November 17, 1941.

However, the United States couldn't be counted on to sit idly by as Japan plunged further into Asia. Committing to the Southern Operation would mean committing to war with the Americans. Success in that war, Japanese planners believed, would require seizing the initiative. Early on, Japan would have to invade the Philippines, the island chain that extended to within 500 miles of southeastern China and that was defended by a combined U.S.-Filipino garrison. The Japanese would also have to neutralize the U.S. Pacific Fleet, which, from its base in Pearl Harbor, Hawaii, would sail to East Asia and join the battle.

Admiral Isoroku Yamamoto, the man who drew the assignment of figuring out how to neutralize American naval power, didn't relish a confrontation with the United States. The 56-year-old career officer had spent enough time in America—first as a student at Harvard University and later as a naval attaché in Washington, D.C.—to appreciate the industrial and military potential of the United States. Still, Yamamoto was a patriot, and as his country moved closer to a showdown with the Americans, he applied his formidable military mind to the problem at hand.

An avid poker player, Yamamoto devised a plan that only a high-stakes gambler could truly appreciate, a plan that involved huge risks—and the possibility of equally huge rewards. The plan called for a massive naval task force, whose core would consist of six aircraft carriers, to sail thousands of miles across the Pacific Ocean, from the Kurile Islands in northern Japan to within a few hundred miles of the Hawaiian island of Oahu. There, undetected, the carriers would launch hundreds of bombers, which would unleash a devastating surprise attack on the U.S. Pacific Fleet as it lay at anchor in Pearl Harbor. The shock produced by the defeat, no less than the actual crippling of U.S. naval forces in the Pacific, would lead the unprepared Americans to ask for a quick peace, leaving Japan to do as it pleased in East Asia.

Initially, many of Japan's military leaders believed that Yamamoto's plan bordered on reckless. The length of the task force's route—some 4,000 miles—was unprecedented in Japanese naval history and would require difficult underway refueling. Plus, the ships would have to maintain total radio silence throughout the voyage to avoid detection. Then, too, there was a more fundamental concern: were aircraft carriers worthy of the central role Yamamoto had assigned them? As of

1941 the flattop, a relatively new innovation in naval warfare, remained largely untested in battle.

On September 6, 1941, Japan's leaders met at an Imperial conference to discuss future relations with the United States. Prime Minister Konoe urged continued negotiation. But the tide had turned in favor of the militarists, whose main spokesman, General Hideki Tojo, argued convincingly that war with the Americans was inevitable, and that initiating it sooner rather than later would work to Japan's benefit. Ultimately Prince Konoe was granted six weeks to obtain an acceptable agreement with the Americans.

Next the conferees considered Yamamoto's plan. Many who had earlier expressed reservations now endorsed the Pearl Harbor attack. Though he stood just 5 feet 2 inches tall, Admiral Yamamoto had immense stature within the Imperial Japanese military. The lifelong warrior, who in 1905 had lost two fingers at the Battle of Tsushima Strait—the greatest of all Japanese naval victories—inspired confidence in his colleagues. Should the need arise, they believed, his plan would give Japan another glorious victory.

But at least one man urged restraint. Vice Admiral Takijiro Onishi feared that rather than shocking the Americans into a quick capitulation, the surprise attack might make them "so insanely mad" that they would stop at nothing short of Japan's complete destruction.

As the decision makers pondered Onishi's warning, another voice was heard. Small and slight, with eyeglasses and a thin mustache, Emperor Hirohito didn't look like a god. But his people venerated him as one, believing that his ancestors had descended from Ameratsu, the sun goddess. By long tradition, the emperor didn't decide policy issues, and in fact Hirohito rarely spoke at these Imperial conferences. Now, however, he seemed to sound a vague note of caution. The vastness of China, he said, had prevented Japan from gaining a final victory, and the Pacific Ocean was even more immense. Still, Yamamoto's plan was approved.

By mid-October, with no progress at the negotiations in Washington, Prince Konoe resigned. General Tojo assumed the position of prime minister. Tojo and his ministers ultimately imposed a deadline of November 29 for a diplomatic breakthrough with the Americans. Three days earlier they put in motion the Pearl Harbor plan. Yamamoto's naval task force, under the command of Vice Admiral Chuichi Nagumo, had set sail from Hitokappu Bay in the remote Kurile Islands. In the event of an 11th-hour agreement with the United States, however, the ships could be recalled.

By the 30th, though, a final decision had been made. Though the Japanese intended to keep up the pretense of negotiating until just before they struck, there would be no turning back now.

A little before 6 A.M. on December 7, Nagumo turned his aircraft carriers into the wind some 200 miles north of Oahu. Amid the buzz and bustle of the flight decks, his pilots scrambled to their planes. Some sported bandannas adorned with the word *Hissho*. Translation: "Certain Victory."

Total War

Framed by thick smoke from raging oil fires are the battleships *West Virginia* (partially sunken in the foreground) and *Tennessee*. Japan's surprise attack on the U.S. Pacific Fleet at Pearl Harbor, Hawaii, on the morning of December 7, 1941, sank or damaged 18 ships, claimed the lives of more than 2,400 American servicemen, and plunged the United States into World War II.

3

A little before 8 A.M. on December 7, 1941, a serene Sunday morning in Hawaii, 183 planes appeared in the skies above Pearl Harbor. Below, in the cluster of military facilities in and around the harbor, no one seemed to notice.

Suddenly bombs and bullets started raining down on the battleships, destroyers, and cruisers of the U.S. Pacific Fleet. Moored, mostly in pairs, around Ford Island in the middle of the harbor, the ships were helpless against the swarm of Imperial Japanese fighters and bombers. Within minutes of the start of the attack, Japanese aviators had scored hits on the *Oklahoma*, *Utah*, *Raleigh*, and *West Virginia*. A bomb that pierced the deck of the *Arizona* exploded in the battleship's forward magazine, detonating tons of ammunition and sending the ship to the bottom with more than

"No matter how long it may take us to overcome this premeditated invasion," President Franklin Delano Roosevelt pledged in asking Congress for a declaration of war against Imperial Japan, "the American people in their righteous might will win through to absolute victory."

1,100 seamen aboard. After the Japanese airplanes had dropped their bombs and strafed the American airfields with machine-gun fire, they flew off—only to be replaced by a second wave of Imperial bombers and fighter planes. By the time the last Japanese aircraft left some two hours after the initial salvo, the Pacific Fleet was in a shambles. Eight battleships were among the 18 U.S. vessels sunk or severely damaged, and more than 180 airplanes had been destroyed on the ground. More important, 2,403 American servicemen had lost their lives, and an additional 1,178 had been wounded.

The surprise attack shocked and enraged America.

On December 8, President Roosevelt appeared before Congress to ask for a declaration of war against Japan. It was overwhelmingly approved. America's isolationism had come to an abrupt end.

Three days later, on December 11, Adolf Hitler made a decision that must surely rank among his largest strategic blunders. Though the Tripartite Pact didn't require it, because Japan had been the attacker rather than the attacked, Nazi Germany declared war on the United States. Fascist Italy followed suit the same day. America would be fighting in two theaters, European and Pacific. Roosevelt decided that the former would receive top priority.

In his speech before Congress on the eighth, however, the president had given voice to a special outrage many Americans now felt toward Japan, auguring the fulfillment of Takijiro Onishi's fears of an "insanely mad" United States. "Always we will remember the character of the onslaught against us," Roosevelt declared. "No matter how long it may take us to overcome this premeditated invasion, the American people in their righteous might will win through to absolute victory."

Yet through the first four months of America's war with Japan, absolute victory seemed anything but certain as the Imperial forces readily achieved one objective after another. Japan extended its control in a wide crescent running from Burma and Southeast Asia south through the Indonesian archipelago, east to New Guinea and the Solomon Islands in the southern Pacific, and north through the central Pacific islands of Wake and Guam. Japan had obtained the vital natural resources its armies needed, and behind its huge defensive perimeter the Japanese home islands seemed safe from attack. Japanese bases on New Guinea might even threaten northern Australia.

American strategy in the event of a war with Japan had called for the U.S. garrison in the Philippine Islands to tie up the Japanese for three or four months. This would prevent Japan's southward expansion and give the U.S. fleet time to cross the Pacific, destroy the Imperial Japanese fleet, and thereby bring the war to a quick conclusion.

Things didn't go according to plan. After he learned of the Japanese attack on Pearl Harbor, U.S. Army chief of staff George C. Marshall, in Washington, called his commander in the Philippines, General Douglas MacArthur. But rather than taking immediate action—or even moving his force of B-17 bombers—MacArthur retreated into his bedroom to read his Bible. Nine hours later, Japanese planes destroyed the B-17s on the ground. The bombers were supposed to have formed the backbone of MacArthur's plan to repel a Japanese invasion.

With control of the air, Japan was able to land soldiers on Luzon, the main island of the Philippines, on December 22. Soon the Japanese took the capital of Manila, and more than 70,000 American and Filipino troops—joined by 26,000 civilians—retreated to the Bataan Peninsula. From his headquarters on the island fortress of Corregidor, just south of the peninsula, MacArthur tried to direct a holding action. Outnumbered, poorly supplied, and weakened by disease, however, the Philippine garrison gradually gave way. Upon orders from President Roosevelt, MacArthur evacuated to Australia on March 12, 1942, to assume command of the Allied forces in the southwestern Pacific.

Lieutenant General Jonathan M. Wainwright drew the unenviable job of taking over the Bataan-Corregidor defense. The situation was in fact hopeless. On April 9 the exhausted Bataan contingent—with the exception of about 3,500 men who escaped to Corregidor—

surrendered. Wainwright, taking refuge from the Japanese bombardment in a tunnel along with thousands of his sick and wounded men, held Corregidor for four more weeks before capitulating.

What happened next would contribute in no small way to the building hatred of American fighting men and their leaders toward the Japanese enemy. The Japanese drove their 70,000 captives on a 65-mile forced march to prisoner-of-war camps at the base of the Bataan Peninsula. The incident would become known as the Bataan Death March, and for good reason. In addition to denying water to the POWs, Japanese soldiers shot, clubbed, bayoneted, and beheaded stragglers. As many as 10,600 Filipino and American prisoners died on the march.

Guarded by their Japanese captors, American soldiers carry sick and wounded comrades during the Bataan Death March. More than 10,000 American and Filipino prisoners died during the 65-mile trek; many were murdered by the victorious Japanese.

Japan's inhuman treatment of captives did not end at Bataan but continued throughout the war. "The record Japan created in her treatment of prisoners of war and civilian internees," the military historian Richard B. Frank has written, "still appalls. Prisoners were starved and brutalized systematically. They were murdered by deadly purpose or on momentary whim. They were beaten to death, beheaded, burned alive, buried alive, crucified, marched to death, shot, stabbed, strangled, and simply abandoned to die." Statistics for U.S. Army personnel captured by Axis forces paint a stark picture of Japanese brutality: only 0.9 percent of those held by Nazi Germany died in captivity, compared with 35 percent held by Imperial Japan.

Part of the reason for this was cultural. The Japanese military lived by the code of *Bushido,* an inheritance from Japan's medieval warrior class, the samurai. Under Bushido, surrender was the highest dishonor. It followed, then, that prisoners of wars—having dishonored themselves by choosing surrender to death—deserved to be treated with contempt. Japan also had not signed the Geneva Convention, an international agreement on the rules of warfare that governed, among other things, permissible weapons, the treatment of POWs, and protection of civilians.

The Japanese weren't alone in stepping outside the norms of warfare, however. In fact, all the major antagonists in World War II would eventually adopt tactics that violated traditional ideas of what was morally acceptable in war, most notably with regard to the treatment of civilians.

War has always exacted a steep toll on civilians. In some cases, the harm is indirect. For example, the social and economic disruptions war causes have often produced mass starvation and disease. In addition, noncombatants living near the battlefront, particularly with the more destructive weapons of modern times, have frequently become unintended casualties. But history is replete with examples of intentional harm being done to civilians. It was not uncommon in ancient times for an entire city—including women and children—to be put to the sword after a successful siege. Widespread rape and enslavement of conquered civilians was also a frequent outcome.

But more enlightened members of society, recognizing that periodic warfare was inevitable, tried to define standards of behavior to minimize its horrors. As early as the fifth century A.D., Augustine of Hippo articulated the requirements for a "just war," and one of them was that noncombatants must not be intentionally targeted. Over the centuries, other thinkers picked up and developed this principle, which eventually became part of the code of warfare in the Western world and was incorporated into the training of officers.

Of course, in the heat of conflict soldiers frequently failed to live up to the ideal. But for the most part the moral obligation to refrain from targeting noncombatants, and the more general goal of minimizing unintentional civilian casualties, guided the actions of conscientious commanders.

That changed dramatically during World War II. This was war on a scale unimaginable even a decade or two before, war that involved not just highly mechanized armies and navies on far-flung battlefields, but all levels of society, including civilians. This was total war. Unlike previous wars, victory in this conflict hinged equally on defeating the enemy in the field and on choking off the production of vital war materiel—tanks and airplanes, submarines and carriers, munitions, steel, and oil—without which the armies and navies couldn't continue to

Luftwaffe bombers pound London, 1940. The Axis countries were first to target civilians through the indiscriminate bombing of cities. But Great Britain and the United States would eventually cross that moral boundary as well.

fight. Thus, destroying enemy factories and transportation systems became as important as killing enemy soldiers, sailors, and airmen. But some commanders took the idea a step further. Destroying the morale of civilians on the home front—civilians who sustained the war effort—might prove as effective as destroying the factories where they worked. And terror, it was felt, could be the key to destroying morale.

Technological advances provided the means of instilling terror. Most significant was the progress in aviation technology. Long-range bombers could fly hundreds or thousands of miles behind the front lines and deliver death and destruction to people who would otherwise have been safe, who would otherwise not experience the horrors of the conflict firsthand.

Germany had pioneered the use of aerial terror bombing during World War I. Its high-flying zeppelins—hydrogen-filled airships—and small Gotha planes had crossed the English Channel to drop bombs on London. But damage and casualties were minimal, and the main effect was to enrage the British populace.

Twenty-odd years later, larger airplanes with longer ranges and bigger payloads made effective terror attacks against civilians feasible. During the 1930s each of the Axis nations gave the world a small taste of what was to come: Italian aviators dropped high explosives and poison gas during Italy's war with Ethiopia, Japan terror-bombed Chungking and other Chinese cities in an effort to crush support for Chiang Kai-shek, and Nazi airmen slaughtered civilians in the city of Guernica as part of Germany's support for Francisco Franco's Nationalists during the Spanish Civil War.

In the first months of World War II, the Nazis replicated these early experiments in aerial intimidation on a larger scale. A fairly limited bombing raid on the city of Rotterdam in May 1940 obtained the surrender of the Dutch commander the next day, prompting Hitler and his generals to try the same tactic to bring England to its knees. Bomber raids destroyed much of London, Coventry, and other English cities, killing thousands of civilians. Later, after the tide of war had begun to turn against them, the Nazis unleashed their *Vergeltungswaffen* ("vengeance weapons") on the English capital. In 1944 these unmanned, jet-propelled rockets, the V-1 and the larger and deadlier V-2, were fired across the English Channel from bases in France and the Low Countries.

Combined they caused 55,000 civilian casualties.

But the Axis nations would be repaid manyfold for changing the norms of warfare by deliberately targeting civilians. At the beginning of the war Great Britain restricted its strategic bombing to daytime "precision" raids on military-industrial targets (though the best technology of the day offered only a limited degree of precision). In the face of huge losses to Nazi air defenses, however, the British quickly abandoned this policy in favor of nighttime bombing. While safer for the British air crews, nighttime bombing was much less accurate. Only one in five bombs dropped at night, a 1941 British report indicated, landed within five miles of its target. Because industrial targets were invariably located in and around cities, the stray bombs were guaranteed to kill a lot of civilians. British commanders were untroubled by this fact. Later, the British would unapologetically adopt the tactics of their Nazi adversaries and deliberately target civilians, in part out of a desire for retribution for the deadly raids on London and other English cities, in part because of the perception that breaking the morale of German citizens was militarily necessary. British air raids on the city of Hamburg in July and August of 1943 clearly reflected the new thinking: of almost 45,000 Germans killed, all but about 800 were civilians.

U.S. doctrine on the use of air power would follow a similar evolution, though American leaders never explicitly endorsed the idea of terror-bombing civilians to destroy their morale. Like Great Britain, America began the war carrying out only daylight precision attacks on vital war industries. Furthermore, the Americans insisted on visual aiming: if cloud cover precluded a bombardier from seeing his target, bombs were not to be dropped. This was to minimize civilian casualties. But American airmen sustained big losses while obtaining scant results, in large part because chronically bad weather over northern Europe prevented visual bombing much of the time. While U.S. Army Air Force officials refused to abandon daytime bombing, in November 1943 they approved the use of radar aiming—a much less accurate method than visual aiming—when weather was poor. They made that decision with the full knowledge that civilian casualties would increase substantially. But there was no debate about the moral ramifications of the decision. In the midst of the pitiless war, an ethical boundary was crossed without much thought. By the end of the war in Europe, British and American aerial bombing would kill at least 300,000 German civilians.

Japanese civilians would suffer an even larger death toll when the fortunes of war turned against their country.

For the Imperial armed forces, the long road to defeat began near Midway Island on June 4, 1942. In the epic naval battle the United States sank four Japanese aircraft carriers while losing only one of its own. The naval balance of power in the Pacific shifted permanently to the American side, and U.S. troops were finally ready to take the offensive.

Years of bloody fighting would be required to shrink Japan's huge defensive perimeter, approach its home islands, and bring the war to an end. America's military planners adopted a two-pronged offensive strategy. Leading the army, General Douglas MacArthur would emerge from Australia to attack Japanese positions in the southwest Pacific, capturing northern New Guinea and proceeding northward through the Indonesian islands toward the Philippines. Leading the marines, Admiral Chester Nimitz, who had assumed command of the U.S. Pacific Fleet after the Pearl Harbor disaster, would island-hop up the central Pacific, using the formidable naval power at his disposal. As he moved north, each successive island group he seized would be used as a forward base for air and naval forces planning the next assault.

Nimitz and his commanders got an indication of just how ferocious the fighting would be during the first engagement of the campaign. On Guadalcanal, in the Solomon Islands, the U.S. Marines needed six months of ferocious jungle fighting to dislodge the Japanese defenders. And for the first time, the Americans saw the flip side of the Bushido ethic. The Japanese had shown themselves to be merciless in victory. Now they proved unyielding in defeat. Only a minuscule number were captured. "I have never heard or read of this kind of fighting," the U.S. Marines commander, Major General Alexander Archer Vandegrift, wrote. "These people refuse to surrender. The wounded wait until men come up to examine them . . . and blow themselves and the other fellow to pieces with a hand grenade."

The Americans would see this kind of fighting again and again as they slowly, and with a great toll in lives lost, reduced Japan's Pacific empire. And as U.S. forces got closer to the home islands, Japanese resistance became even more fanatical.

More than 71,000 U.S. troops landed on the island of Saipan, in the Marianas chain, in June 1944. Before the three-week struggle for the island was over, more than 14,000 would become casualties, a rate of almost 20 percent. All but 3 percent of the 30,000 Japanese soldiers fought to the death.

On Saipan, for the first time in the Pacific campaign, the Americans also encountered a sizable civilian population. In a development that shocked even the marines, whole families of Japanese civilians—children included— threw themselves off cliffs or blew themselves up with grenades rather than suffer capture at the hands of the Americans.

Three months later, at the huge naval battle of Leyte Gulf in the Philippines, the Americans were in for another shock. Though defeated decisively in the engagement, the Japanese systematically deployed a new and terrifying weapon: the kamikaze. These suicide pilots tried to crash their explosive-laden planes directly into American ships. At Leyte Gulf the kamikazes scored several hits, one of which blew up the escort carrier *St. Lô* and killed 114 American sailors.

The taking of the Marianas had put U.S. bombers within easy reach of the Japanese homeland, and a month after the kamikazes made their first appearance at Leyte Gulf, the Army Air Force's 21st Bomber Command was ready to launch its initial strike. The unit's commander, Brigadier General Haywood Hansell, had a fearsome

U.S. Marines on the beach at Saipan, June 1944. During the three-week struggle for the island, 97 percent of the Japanese defenders fought to the death— inflicting a casualty rate of almost 20 percent on the Americans. The fanaticism of soldiers and civilians alike alarmed American commanders planning an invasion of the Japanese home islands.

Emperor Hirohito tours a section of Tokyo destroyed in an American bombing raid. The March 9, 1945, fire-bombing of the Japanese capital burned out nearly 16 square miles and killed 90,000 to 100,000 people, mostly civilians—a stark reminder of the pitiless nature of total war.

new weapon at his disposal: the B-29 "Superfortress." Almost 100 feet long, with a wingspan measuring 141 feet, the Superfortress could fly 4,000 miles and deliver up to 20,000 pounds of bombs.

But Hansell's command was plagued with problems. His unit sustained heavy losses and flew mission after mission in vain attempts to destroy the same targets. Part of the reason for Hansell's failure to get results was that his pilots were flying near the operational ceiling of the B-29—35,000 feet. At that altitude the jet stream, a powerful current of wind, blew the bombs off target. But a more significant factor was Hansell's insistence on holding to the ethical standards that had until only recently prevailed. Despite pressure from his superiors, Hansell remained firmly committed to minimizing civilian casualties by undertaking only precision bombing.

That commitment cost him his command. On January 6, 1945, he was relieved of duty. In three months he'd failed to destroy a single high-priority target.

Hansell's replacement as head of the 21st Bomber Command was Curtis E. LeMay. One of the army's youngest generals, the gruff, bearlike LeMay didn't share the qualms of his predecessor. "I'll tell you what war is about," he once declared. "You've got to kill people, and when you've killed enough, they stop fighting."

LeMay soon changed the 21st Bomber Command's tactics. They were going to fly low and they weren't going to worry about precision. They were, in fact, going to set out to destroy wide swaths of Japanese cities, not particular ball-bearing factories or aircraft-engine plants or munitions storage facilities within those cities. Technically, the targets would still be military-industrial, because Japan had dispersed its wartime production and used a feeder system to supply its larger factories. Under the feeder system, component parts such as shell fuses were manufactured in private homes near a factory and then sent on to be assembled into weapons at the factory. LeMay realized that this provided "a pretty thin veneer" for justifying the destruction of houses—which, obviously, would have people inside. In fact, the real targets of his raids would be civilians, including women and children. Another moral boundary was about to be crossed. "Had to be done," LeMay said laconically.

With the ethical issues disposed of, there remained the question of what was the most efficient way to get the job done. LeMay realized that Japanese cities, with their houses constructed of wood and paper, were especially vulnerable to fire. Instead of dropping large, high-explosive bombs, he decided to rely primarily on an incendiary, or fire-producing bomb. The M-69, a six-pound device, was dropped in 500-pound, grapelike clusters. The individual bombs would detach from the cluster as it approached the ground. When a bomb hit, a charge would send a stream of napalm—gelatinized gasoline that clung to whatever it touched—out the tail section. Moments later, another charge would ignite the napalm.

On the night of March 9, 1945, LeMay dispatched 334 Superfortresses from the Marianas. Their destination was a residential district of Tokyo called Shitamachi. Arriving just after midnight, the first planes laid down a large, flaming X that guided the other planes to the target. Soon M-69s were falling like a sheet of silver rain, and small fires were bubbling up everywhere. Fueled by all the wood and paper from the houses, and fanned by 15-mile-per-hour winds, the fire spread rapidly into a huge conflagration.

Terrified residents raced to escape the inferno. Many burned to death in collapsing houses. Others asphyxiated because the fire was so large that it consumed all the oxygen in the area. Still others jumped into ponds and canals, not realizing that the heat from the conflagration had set the water boiling.

All told, LeMay's four-hour raid killed 90,000 to 100,000 Japanese citizens and injured an additional one million. A million people were also left homeless as nearly 16 square miles of Tokyo burned down.

Over the next months, the 21st Bomber Command would unleash firestorms in dozens of other Japanese cities, killing as many as 700,000 persons. Though the damage and casualties were truly appalling, Curtis LeMay stayed resolved in his purpose. If he didn't carry out his gruesome task, his superiors had informed him, an invasion of Japan would be necessary. And that might entail enormous American casualties. As the general later explained with characteristic bluntness, "We're at war with Japan. . . . Do you want to kill Japanese, or would you rather have Americans killed?"

Decisions

Harry S. Truman takes the presidential oath of office following the death of President Roosevelt, April 12, 1945. Minutes after the swearing-in ceremony, Truman first heard about a secret program to develop a new type of weapon.

4

O n April 12, 1945, President Franklin Delano Roosevelt died in Warm Springs, Georgia, of a massive cerebral hemorrhage. His vice president, Harry S. Truman, took the presidential oath of office at 7:09 that evening, becoming America's 33rd chief executive.

Minutes after the ceremony, Truman heard, for the first time, about a program to create a new type of weapon. But the cabinet official briefing him, Secretary of War Henry L. Stimson, was so vague that Truman couldn't figure out what he was talking about. The following day Jimmy Byrnes, a Roosevelt confidant whom Truman would make his secretary of state, briefed the new president more thoroughly on the program that had been code-named the Manhattan Project.

Since mid-1942, at facilities spread across the country, the United

States had been at work on producing a bomb that would rely not on a chemical reaction, like conventional high explosives, but on a nuclear one. If the idea proved to be workable, the weapon might generate a blast many times more powerful than that produced by any previous weapon. General Leslie R. Groves had been placed in overall command of the Manhattan Project. Groves, in turn, had selected a young physicist named J. Robert Oppenheimer to head up the main scientific research and technical work, from a facility in remote Los Alamos, New Mexico. By 1945 the enormous theoretical, technical, and industrial hurdles inherent in the project had swelled its total workforce to more than 100,000 persons nationwide.

The origins of the whole massive undertaking could be traced to a discovery—little noticed outside a small circle of elite theoretical physicists—made by two Germans in 1938. Bombarding the radioactive element uranium with neutrons, tiny particles found in the nuclei of atoms, Otto Hahn and Fritz Strassmann were left with small quantities of a different element, barium. It remained for two more German scientists, Lise Meitner and Otto Frisch, to figure out the meaning of this strange transformation: despite the conventional belief that atoms were indivisible, Hahn and Strassmann had split the nuclei of uranium atoms in two. This process is called fission.

Follow-up experiments showed that the two fragments of a split nucleus repel each other with tremendous force—releasing up to 100 million times more energy than is released in a chemical reaction of the same size. They also showed that each atom fissioned releases two or three neutrons, which can in turn fission two or three additional atoms. With each successive generation of fissions, the number of neutrons released, and hence the number of new fissions, increases exponentially—until the force created by the fission process pushes apart the uranium and stops the reaction. A fission reaction can occur only when the fissionable material is densely packed.

A few people grasped the military implications. If a way could be devised to bring together enough uranium and keep it together through a chain reaction involving many generations of fission events, near the end of that reaction a large number of atoms would be fissioning simultaneously. The result would be an explosion of immense destructiveness.

In the early months of the war the Nazis began a secret atomic bomb program, led by the Nobel Prize–winning physicist Werner Heisenberg and including such luminaries as Otto Hahn, the codiscoverer of fission. The worried British initiated their own program and pleaded with the Americans to throw their scientific and industrial resources into the effort. Although President Roosevelt authorized funding for research in late 1941, it wasn't until the following year that a full-scale effort to build the bomb got under way with the creation of the Manhattan Project.

In 1942 Japan, too, entered the race to construct an atomic bomb. Dr. Yoshio Nishina, a 52-year-old physicist who had founded the Nuclear Research Laboratory at Tokyo's Riken Institute, was picked to lead the Japanese program. By order of Prime Minister Hideki Tojo, Nishina enjoyed unlimited resources to develop the Japanese atom bomb.

Otto Hahn, the co-discoverer of fission, was among the eminent German scientists who lent their expertise to Nazi Germany's program to develop an atomic bomb.

Neither Japan nor Germany would come close to solving the theoretical and technical problems associated with developing the atom bomb, however. The only nation that might possibly possess the new weapon by war's end—and hence the only nation that might have to decide what to do with it—was the United States. Ultimately the decision would fall on the shoulders of President Truman.

Within a month of the new president's taking office, Nazi Germany surrendered. All attention now shifted to the war in the Pacific.

The outcome of that war had long ago been decided. Imperial Japan had lost, but it continued the fight anyway. With the American scientists predicting that an atomic bomb would be ready for testing by midsummer, the situation was rapidly coming to a head.

Some Manhattan Project scientists had already expressed grave reservations about their work. They shuddered at the thought of annihilating thousands of civilians with a uranium bomb. They also worried that using the bomb would usher in a new and unspeakably horrifying era in warfare. Oppenheimer, their leader, didn't share this concern. The atomic bomb, he said, "is a weapon which has no military significance" beyond making "a very big bang." If dropped on a city, he predicted, it might kill 20,000 people. But of course dropping tons of high-explosive bombs or incendiaries would produce the same results.

Oppenheimer and other Manhattan Project scientists guessed that the first atomic bomb available might produce the explosive power of about 5 kilotons, or 5,000 tons, of dynamite. (The actual yield turned out to be two and a half times larger.) There was a certain historical irony in this measurement. Alfred Nobel, the Swedish chemist who in 1867 patented dynamite—also called

TNT—recoiled at the thought of his invention being used in warfare. But Nobel hoped that the destructive power of TNT would ultimately bring peace, because war would become too horrible to be waged. That hadn't happened, and now weapons capable of producing as much destruction as thousands of tons of dynamite were under development.

In addition to its powerful blast effects, Manhattan Project physicists knew that an atomic bomb would release deadly radiation, which they estimated would extend to a radius of perhaps two-thirds of a mile. Because they believed that anyone within this range would be killed immediately in the blast, they considered the radiation effects irrelevant.

Still, some scientists and government officials argued for a so-called peaceful demonstration of the atomic

Part of the Oak Ridge, Tennessee, complex where U235 was separated for use in an atomic bomb. The Manhattan Project, a scientific and industrial effort unparalleled in history, consumed $2 billion and employed more than 100,000 workers nationwide.

bomb before it was used against Japan. Perhaps represen-
tatives from the world's nations, including Japan, could
be invited to witness the test in the summer. After the
awesome display, Japan would recognize the hopeless-
ness of its situation and surrender. But what if the test
failed? critics of the proposal asked. Wouldn't that simply embolden Imperial leaders?

Another proposal called for warning the Japanese
before demonstrating the bomb on a city. That would
allow an evacuation, sparing civilian lives, but would still
permit the bomb's power to be graphically demonstrated.
The rejoinder: God help the pilot and crew if the Japanese knew where they were going to strike. Still another
option involved striking without warning an uninhabited
target. One person suggested blowing the top off Mount
Fuji, a dormant volcano considered sacred in Japan. But
given that the United States would have only enough uranium and plutonium (a man-made element suitable for a
fission weapon) after the summer test for two bombs,
such a demonstration was considered extravagant.

Besides, argued General Groves and others, all the
peaceful-demonstration options missed the point. The
bomb was intended to shock the Imperial leadership and
the Japanese people into submission. Giving them any
prior notice of the existence or properties of the bomb
would just lessen its shock value and reduce the likeli-
hood of a surrender.

Given all the possible options and the enormity of the
stakes, one might assume that President Truman ago-
nized over his decision about what to do with the atomic
bomb. All evidence suggests that he didn't. After he was
informed of the successful test near Alamogordo on July
16, Truman authorized a combat drop on a Japanese city
as soon as the army was ready.

Truman's decision, one of the most momentous of

the entire 20th century, is also one of the most controversial. Postwar critics have suggested that dropping the atomic bomb was militarily unnecessary. By midsummer, they insist, Japan was on the verge of surrender. A planned invasion of the home islands would have brought the war to a speedy conclusion, and it would have been a more humane option, these critics argue. Furthermore, they say—citing low casualty estimates that were floating around in 1945—an invasion wouldn't

HOW THE LITTLE BOY URANIUM BOMB WORKED

In nature the metallic element uranium (U) occurs in three different forms, or isotopes: U234, U235, and U238. Typically all three isotopes are mixed together in the ore from which uranium is extracted, but in unequal proportions. U238 makes up about 99.3 percent of naturally occurring uranium; U235, about 0.7 percent. Only trace amounts of U234 exist.

Because only U235 is useful for an atomic bomb, scientists had to separate that isotope from naturally occurring uranium, a laborious process. By 1945—three years into the Manhattan Project—enough purified U235 was available for just one bomb. (Anticipating this problem, however, Oppenheimer's team had also designed a bomb that used the element plutonium, produced in nuclear reactors from U238.)

Spontaneous fissions may occur within a small sample of purified U235, but these fission events won't be numerous enough to cause a chain reaction. In other words, after a few random fissions the process will stop. But with a large enough amount of U235—called a critical mass—a chain reaction will result. An initial generation of fissions will lead to a larger second generation, an even larger third, and so on in a geometrically expanding chain. The process will end only when an explosion blows apart the uranium.

Inside the steel housing of the uranium bomb, dubbed Little Boy, was a tube, at opposite ends of which were two subcritical pieces of U235. One piece resembled a somewhat rounded bullet; the other consisted of rings. High explosives fired the bullet at an extremely fast rate down the tube and into the rings. Once the two pieces were thus assembled, the U235 reached critical mass, chain-reacted, and, within a fraction of a second, produced a massive explosion.

Marines use flamethrowers against Japanese positions on Iwo Jima, a volcanic island 660 miles from Tokyo, March 4, 1945. The Japanese garrison had constructed a maze of tunnels and caves—effective defenses that Imperial commanders began replicating on the home island of Kyushu, where a planned U.S. invasion was slated to begin November 1.

have been unacceptably costly in American lives. According to Truman's harshest critics, the decision to drop the atomic bomb was really motivated by the president's desire to intimidate the Soviet Union.

It is true that conflicts between the Soviets and the West had already begun to emerge by 1945. In addition, the evidence suggests that Secretary of State Jimmy Byrnes, and probably Truman as well, believed that a demonstration of the bomb's power might make Joseph Stalin a bit more cooperative. But supporters of the president's decision, including many historians, insist that Truman saw this as a bonus; it was not, they say, his primary reason for ordering the use of the atomic bomb.

Truman himself would always insist that his primary consideration had been to save American lives. Supporters have found the evidence sufficient to take the president—a former World War I artillery captain beloved by

his troops because he didn't lose a single man in combat—at his word. While critics can point to some
wartime sources who believed that Japan was close to
surrender, and some relatively low casualty estimates for
an invasion, by no means was such optimism universal.
In fact, in the most recent American campaigns, at Iwo
Jima and Okinawa, the Japanese had inflicted horren-
dous casualties on the U.S. forces in some of the most
ferocious fighting of the entire war. Kamikaze missions
had multiplied. And Okinawa and Iwo Jima were still
hundreds of miles from Japan's home islands. It would
not have been unreasonable to expect even more fanatical
resistance in defense of the Japanese heartland.

American military planners had devised a two-phase
campaign to finally bring the war to an end. During the
first stage, dubbed Operation Olympic, more than three-
quarters of a million ground troops, supported by abundant naval and air power, would be committed to seizing
the southernmost of Japan's home islands, Kyushu.
Olympic was scheduled to begin on November 1, 1945.
After storming ashore at the few suitable landing areas
the rocky, mountainous island afforded, the troops would
fight their way inland and sweep northward through narrow valleys until they had pushed the Japanese defenders
off the island. At that point, Kyushu would be used as a
forward base for supplies and air support for the second
and final stage of the campaign, Operation Coronet.

Coronet envisioned an even larger amphibious invasion of Honshu, Japan's main island, at the Kanto Plain.
More than one million troops would be committed to the
operation. Tentatively scheduled to begin March 1, 1946,
its initial objective would be to subdue the Yokohama-
Tokyo area, Japan's industrial, governmental, and
symbolic center. After that, the invasion forces would
sweep across Honshu and quell further resistance as

necessary. With luck, fighting would cease by late spring.

American casualty estimates for the combined Olympic and Coronet operations varied widely according to the source. In Washington, D.C., the Joint Staff Planners (a group that ranked just below the Joint Chiefs of Staff) offered a lower-end estimate of 193,500 casualties, including 43,500 dead, before eventually deciding that accurate estimates weren't possible given the unpredictability of Japanese resistance. At the higher end, a formula developed by the army's surgeon general on the basis of previous amphibious campaigns against the Japanese projected 1,202,005 casualties, including 314,619 killed and missing, if both Olympic and Coronet lasted three months. On several occasions Truman requested a firm casualty estimate for the invasion of Japan, but his military advisers never gave him an unambiguous reply. This, the president's supporters maintain, completely undercuts the critics' argument that Truman knew the war could be ended with a minimum of American bloodshed and without resorting to an atomic-bomb drop.

Supporters and critics alike often fail to consider two key points about Truman's decision. First, the president cannot have known precisely the destruction the atomic bomb would wreak, when even the scientists who had created it were unsure. Second, and more fundamentally, by the summer of 1945 the appropriateness of obliterating a city and slaughtering its inhabitants was no longer questioned. In the cauldron of total war, that consideration had long ago disappeared. Having a military or industrial target for an aiming point was all commanders still insisted on.

Truman's decision remains the most scrutinized, but the decisions made by leaders in Tokyo shaped the tragic events of the summer of 1945 as well. As the year opened, it was clear that Japan had no chance of defeating the

United States. But the Imperial government and its military leaders believed they could still find a way to avoid the ultimate dishonor of surrendering.

The plan they developed reflected both their increasing desperation and a gross miscalculation of the will of their enemy. Since before Pearl Harbor, Japanese leaders had been denigrating Americans as products of a liberal, individualistic society who would never have the stomach for a bloody and protracted conflict. That assessment had not been borne out, reasonable observers would probably agree, but it formed the basis of the new Japanese strategy. Quite simply, that strategy entailed inflicting casualties so appalling that America would lose the will to fight any further. Then Japan could dictate terms it found acceptable to end the hostilities, or at least it could negotiate acceptable terms with the United States. In any event, surrender would be avoided.

The site of the final, appallingly bloody battle, Emperor Hirohito acknowledged in a directive published on January 20, would be the Japanese homeland itself. Thus was born *Ketsu-Go,* the "Decisive" Operation. On the home island of Kyushu, where the Japanese commanders correctly deduced the initial American assault would come, feverish preparations for the upcoming battle began.

The Americans held a decided advantage in firepower, but the *Ketsu-Go* strategy envisioned neutralizing that edge through *tokko* (special attack or suicide) tactics. Kamikaze pilots would dive into troop transport ships, of course, with suicide minisubs and suicide swimmers supplementing the effort. But once the Americans had landed and begun to move inland, swarms of fighters would throw themselves at the invaders, hoping to exchange their life for the life of an American. A large number of these fighters would come from the ranks of

Prince Fumimaro Konoe, appointed as Emperor Hirohito's personal emissary to Moscow in July 1945, never got the chance to ask the Soviet Union to mediate a negotiated settlement with the United States.

civilians: by order of the Japanese cabinet, all men ages 15 to 60, and all women ages 17 to 40, were to be mobilized for *Ketsu-Go*. With its depleted resources, Japan couldn't arm these civilian units very well. Many wielded spears or sharpened tools. But for what they were being asked to do, that might suffice. A mobilized high school girl who'd been issued an awl (a hand tool for boring holes) recalled being told, "Even killing just one American soldier will do. You must prepare to use the awls for self-defense. You must aim at the enemy's abdomen." Whether or not such tactics would kill many marines, one thing is certain: the militarists who still controlled Japan were prepared to sacrifice a frightening number of their civilian countrymen—and women and young people—to avoid having to surrender.

In April a new Japanese cabinet was formed, and two of its members, Prime Minister Baron Kantaro Suzuki and Foreign Minister Shigenori Togo, were moderates who favored exploring roads to peace other than the *Ketsu-Go* strategy. But neither man seemed to be in any great rush. In May, Togo began pursuing the possibility of enlisting Soviet aid in mediating a peace accord with the Americans, but the diplomatic approach was tentative and ultimately produced no results. Meanwhile Army Minister Korechika Anami vehemently insisted that any peace plan reflect the fact

that Japan had not been defeated and was still in possession of a large empire. Acceptable peace conditions
would allow for the Japanese army to withdraw from its
overseas territories as it prescribed, and maybe even for
Japan to retain some of those territories.

In July, Emperor Hirohito decided to send his own
special envoy, Prince Konoe, to Moscow. Though this
uncharacteristic Imperial intervention in affairs of state
reflected Hirohito's conviction that the war must be
ended, he apparently lacked a sense of urgency to push
for a Japanese surrender. Konoe's mission also would be
to obtain the Soviets' help in getting a face-saving agreement with the Americans. The special envoy would
depart for the Soviet Union only after the diplomatic
groundwork had been laid, which might take weeks. But
time was in fact running out for Japan.

One person who apparently grasped the urgency of
the situation was Naotake Sato, a former foreign minister
who now served as Japan's diplomatic representative
in Moscow. Sato had no illusions that the diplomatic
approaches to the Soviets would bear fruit. He implored
Foreign Minister Togo to push for surrender. In a July 8
cable to Togo, he outlined his assessment of the situation
in no uncertain terms: "Except for the matter of mainte-
nance of our national structure [that is, the Imperial
system], I think that we must absolutely not propose
any conditions. The situation has already reached the
point where we have no alternative but unconditional
surrender or its equivalent."

Because American cryptanalysts had broken the
Japanese diplomatic code, they read this message. They
also read Togo's July 21 reply:

> With regard to unconditional surrender we are unable
> to consent to it under any circumstances whatever.

The "Big Three"—from left, British prime minister Winston Churchill, U.S. president Harry Truman, and Soviet premier Joseph Stalin—at the Potsdam Conference. At Truman's insistence, the Potsdam Declaration, which called on Japan to surrender unconditionally, omitted any guarantee of the emperor's future status—an omission, critics charge, that made the tragedy of Hiroshima inevitable.

Even if the war drags on and it becomes clear that it will take much more than bloodshed, the whole country as one man will pit itself against the enemy in accordance with the Imperial Will so long as the enemy demands unconditional surrender.

Franklin Roosevelt had announced the Allies' requirement that their German, Italian, and Japanese adversaries surrender without conditions all the way back in January 1943, at the Casablanca Conference. Though Roosevelt's statement had come as a surprise to the British and the Russians, they quickly endorsed the idea of unconditional surrender. The reason was not simply vindictiveness. The Allies saw an object lesson in the conclusion of the First World War, when Germany was allowed to sign an armistice rather than surrender unconditionally. The German people never knew that their armies had been defeated on the battlefield, and Adolf Hitler was later able to rise to power with claims that Germany had been sold out on the home front by liberals and Jews. After fighting the most horrific war in the history of humanity, the United States and Great Britain found themselves only a generation later fighting the same enemy in an even more horrific war. They were determined not to see that happen again. Unconditional surrender would discredit the militarists and allow the Allies to occupy Germany and Japan in order to reform those societies along democratic lines.

On July 26, 1945, from the Potsdam Conference in occupied Germany, the United States and Great Britain, along with China, essentially announced that they were staying the course Roosevelt had charted. Although the Potsdam Declaration guaranteed Japan peace terms that were far more generous than those offered to Nazi Germany, it also said, "We call upon the government of Japan to proclaim now the unconditional surrender of all Japanese armed forces."

"[F]or the enemy to say something like that," Prime Minister Suzuki opined on July 30, "means circumstances have arisen that force them also to end the war. That is why they are talking about unconditional surrender. Precisely at a time like this, if we hold firm, they will yield before we do."

"No longer a city, but a burnt-over prairie." Only buildings of reinforced concrete, such as the Hiroshima Prefecture Industrial Promotion Hall (at right), survived the atomic bomb blast and subsequent conflagration.

Metropolis of Death

At the southwestern end of Honshu the river Ota, flowing south, branches out into seven smaller rivers. Across the six delta islands separated by those rivers sprawls the city of Hiroshima. The name, bestowed in the 16th century by a feudal lord who built a castle in the area, well reflects the local geography: Hiro means "wide" or "broad"; shima, "island." More poetically the beautiful city, which is rimmed on three sides by mountains, was called "the Metropolis of Water." To its inhabitants Hiroshima's abundant water represented life.

The capital of Hiroshima Prefecture (a prefecture is roughly akin to an American state), the city was Japan's seventh largest, though its precise population in 1945 is unknown. Some estimates put the civilian population at 280,000 to 290,000.

These civilians were joined by about 43,000 soldiers, making the city a significant military center. Indeed, Hiroshima served as the headquarters of the Japanese Second General Army, which was responsible for the defense of Kyushu against American invasion. In addition, its harbor on the Inland Sea made Hiroshima a major point of embarkation for troops and supplies.

Despite its importance to the Imperial war effort, Hiroshima was, by the summer of 1945, one of the few Japanese cities that Curtis LeMay's B-29s had not set ablaze. Residents expected that to change soon. That was why tens of thousands had evacuated the city for the relative safety of the countryside. That was also why the military authorities had ordered thousands of homes to be razed for firebreaks. The hope was that when the inevitable visit by the Superfortresses occurred, the fires could be contained to individual neighborhoods.

Many Hiroshimans would later measure the passage of time from August 6, 1945. On that date—day one of a terrible new reality—the old world they had known came to a cataclysmic end. But the morning began unremarkably. "The hour was early; the morning still, warm, and beautiful," recorded Dr. Michihiko Hachiya, director of the Hiroshima Communications Hospital, in the diary he maintained between August 6 and September 30. "Shimmering leaves, reflecting sunlight from a cloudless sky, made a pleasant contrast with shadows in my garden as I gazed absently through wide-flung doors opening to the south."

Earlier in the morning, at 7:09, a lone B-29 had appeared over the city, triggering an air raid alert. Residents took cover in shelters. But at 7:31, after the plane flew off, a long siren wailed, signaling the all clear. Believing the situation safe, Hiroshimans from all walks of life went about their daily business.

Miss Katsuko Horibe, an 18-year-old teacher, arrived early at the Honkawa Elementary School for a faculty meeting scheduled for 8:30. The school was located only a few hundred yards southwest of the Aioi Bridge, a T-shaped span at the confluence of the Honkawa and Motoyasu Rivers. The bridge, which was at the very heart of Hiroshima, connected the east and west with the south of the city.

Less than a mile northeast of the Aioi Bridge, Dr. Hachiya lounged around at his house, clad in his under-wear. In a short time he would have to get dressed and walk or bicycle the several hundred yards to his beloved Communications Hospital. A reinforced-concrete struc-ture adjoining the main office of the Communications Bureau, Dr. Hachiya's hospital was only about one-fifth the size of the 600-bed Red Cross Hospital, Hiroshima's largest. But it had a very focused mission: to serve Hiroshima-area employees of the Ministry of Communi-cations—postal, telegraph, and telephone workers—along with their families.

Taeko Teramae was one such employee. Taeko, a 15-year-old student, worked as a part-time switchboard operator at Hiroshima's telephone exchange. She was on duty at the exchange on the morning of August 6.

About a mile south and slightly to the east of the Communications Hospital, Mrs. Sakae Ito stood on Hijiyama Hill. The 34-year-old woman was deputy leader of a group of neighbors, some 40 strong, whom the military authorities had assigned the task of razing houses for firebreaks. All told, about 10,000 citizens of Hiroshima were working on firebreaks on August 6. These included more than 8,000 junior high students, most of whom were assigned to the downtown district.

Reverend Kiyoshi Tanimoto was in suburban Koi, about two miles from downtown Hiroshima, on the morning of the sixth. Mr. Tanimoto, a Methodist minister and chairman of his local neighborhood association, had long been worried about a B-29 raid on the city. When a wealthy manufacturer of his acquaintance had offered to allow friends to store belongings at his unoccupied estate in Koi, Mr. Tanimoto had leaped at the opportunity. He moved everything he could from his church: Bibles, hymnals, altar adornments, an organ, a piano. On this day he was helping a friend move some of the friend's daughter's possessions to the estate. The two men had stopped to rest when, at about 10 minutes past eight, three B-29s were spotted over Hiroshima.

Curiosity more than fear gripped most Hiroshimans who saw the Superfortresses gleaming silver in the morning sun, for such a small number of planes could hardly unleash a major attack. When parachutes opened below the two trailing planes more than 30,000 feet above the city, a group of soldiers on the outskirts of Hiroshima broke into a cheer. They believed the B-29s had been hit and the crews were bailing out. In reality, scientific instruments, not American airmen, were tethered to the parachutes. Those instruments would measure the effects of the deadly cargo that the lead plane, the *Enola Gay,* was about to deliver.

At 8:15 the doors of the *Enola Gay*'s bomb bay opened, releasing Little Boy, a 9,000-pound uranium bomb. Forty-three seconds later, high explosives inside the bomb fired the uranium bullet into the target rings of uranium at the opposite end of the bomb, initiating the nuclear chain reaction.

Bombardier Thomas Ferebee's aiming point had been the Aioi Bridge, but he missed to the southeast by 550 to 800 feet. Little Boy detonated above the courtyard of the Shima Surgical Hospital, at an altitude of about 1,900 feet. The time was 8:16:02.

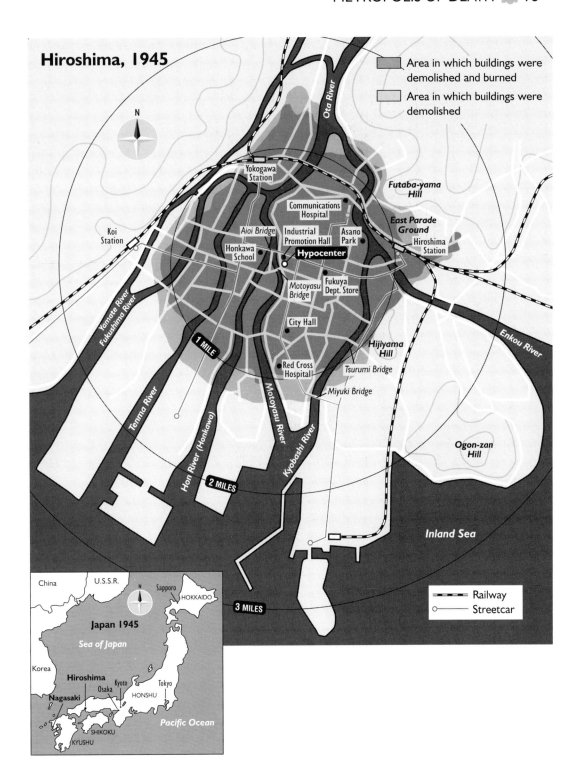

Hiroshima, 1945

Area in which buildings were demolished and burned

Area in which buildings were demolished

N

Ota River

Yokogawa Station

Communications Hospital

Futaba-yama Hill

East Parade Ground

Aioi Bridge

Industrial Promotion Hall

Asano Park

Hiroshima Station

Koi Station

Honkawa School

Hypocenter

Motoyasu Bridge

Fukuya Dept. Store

Yamate River

Fukushima River

City Hall

Hijiyama Hill

Enkou River

1 MILE

Tsurumi Bridge

Red Cross Hospital

Miyuki Bridge

Tenma River

Hon River (Honkawa)

Motoyasu River

Kyobashi River

Ogon-zan Hill

2 MILES

Inland Sea

3 MILES

Railway

Streetcar

China

U.S.S.R.

N

Sapporo

HOKKAIDO

Japan 1945

Sea of Japan

Korea

Hiroshima

Osaka   Kyoto   Tokyo

HONSHU

Nagasaki

SHIKOKU

KYUSHU

Pacific Ocean

A brilliant burst of light—which citizens of Hiroshima would call the *pika,* the Japanese word for "flash"—was the first telltale sign of a large fission reaction. A second later, a fireball expanded to a diameter of 840 feet, and heat rays of up to 5,400°F radiated outward. Also expanding outward, though at the considerably slower rate of 2.8 miles per second, was the shock wave produced by the enormous blast—which was later estimated to be equivalent to 12,500 tons of dynamite. That shock wave would level all wooden structures within a radius of about a mile and a quarter and damage buildings much farther away. More significant, however, was what the bomb did to people.

In an instant, tens of thousands of human beings were killed. The closer a person was to the hypocenter—the point on the ground directly underneath the bomb when it exploded—the greater his or her chance of being one of these victims. Within a radius of a hundred or so yards of the hypocenter, no one survived. The intense heat of the bomb transformed solid objects, such as animals, buildings, trees—and people—into gases; in other words, it vaporized them. In some cases the incredibly bright flash had seared shadowy images of people who no longer existed into stone and pavement, like ghastly photographs. All that remained of one person was a shadow on the granite steps of a bank; the silhouette of another man pulling a cart was preserved on the burnt asphalt of a bridge.

Half a mile away from the hypocenter, only a bit more remained of what had just moments before been flesh-and-blood men, women, and children. The skin of people who were out-of-doors and exposed directly to the rays of the fireball became carbonized and their internal organs evaporated, leaving only small piles of smoking char. Up to a distance of sixth-tenths of a mile from the

Though weighing only 9,000 pounds, the Little Boy atomic bomb (shown here) produced an explosive yield equal to about 12,500 tons—25 million pounds—of dynamite.

hypocenter, 9 of every 10 people who were outside at the moment of the explosion died.

Honkawa Elementary School lay well within that death-filled radius: it was just 650 feet from the hypocenter. But Katsuko Horibe had the good fortune to be inside the sturdy school, which was constructed of reinforced concrete and surrounded by a brick wall. In the faculty room Miss Horibe saw everything around her suddenly suffused with a brilliant bluish light. Almost simultaneously, the windows of the school shattered, and flying glass pierced the forehead, scalp, and arm of the 18-year-old schoolteacher. Everything went black and silent.

As she staggered out of the school building, Miss

Horibe stepped into a hellish scene. Though it was morning, a pall of darkness hung over the city because the atomic explosion had produced a huge mushroom cloud that rose skyward and blocked the sunlight. Closer to the ground, black clouds of dust and smoke swirled wildly, and everything seemed to be on fire. On the playground, seven Honkawa students, burned and bleeding, their uniforms in tatters and strips of skin hanging from their bodies, lay crying in agony. The children had been playing hide-and-seek when the bomb found them. With fires closing in, Miss Horibe tried to rally them to move. "To the river," she exhorted. "It's the only way out."

Though horribly stricken, the students obeyed. The Honkawa River was only a few yards from the school yard, but the small group's progress proved extremely slow. The blast had demolished everything but Hiroshima's strongest buildings—those made of reinforced concrete. Piles of rubble seemed to block the path at every turn.

Finally Miss Horibe's group reached the edge of the Honkawa, which was bordered by a seven-foot-high seawall. But there the teacher became separated from her young charges as a crowd of other dazed and burned survivors surged down the seawall steps toward the water. Miss Horibe never saw any of the children again.

The river, it turned out, offered no escape. It was, in fact, burning—or at least the debris that clogged the river was on fire. Because she had been among the first to arrive, Miss Horibe was able to claim a spot on the rocky, four-foot-wide strip at the water's edge. Pressed close together with the others who had reached the rock beach—most horribly burned on the face and body, many dying, and more than a few already dead—the young schoolteacher gradually became aware of her own condition. Blood was caked on her skin and clothes, she

was starting to feel intense pain, and, like thousands of others in the city that day, she began to repeatedly vomit a yellow liquid.

As fires pressed closer from the direction of the ruined Honkawa Elementary School, some people jumped or were pushed into the river from the seawall seven feet above Miss Horibe's spot on the rocks. But these people's chances of surviving amid the burning debris seemed slim, and most of the bodies floating down-stream appeared dead. With fire behind her and fire in front of her, Miss Horibe herself could see no way out.

This photograph, which shows a cloud rising 20,000 feet over the destroyed city of Hiroshima, was taken about one hour after Little Boy had detonated.

In Hiroshima and later Nagasaki (where this photo was taken), the silhouettes of vaporized human beings were preserved on asphalt, concrete, and other materials. The people's bodies blocked the light and heat rays that radiated outward from the hypocenter, preventing the area of their shadows from being seared like the surrounding surfaces.

At around the time Miss Horibe began to believe her life would end on the banks of the Honkawa River, Taeko Teramae faced a perilous choice on the banks of another river, the Kyobashi. Taeko, the 15-year-old student who worked part-time as a switchboard operator, had been almost three times farther away from the hypocenter than Miss Horibe. And, like the schoolteacher, she had been fortunate to be inside a reinforced-concrete building when the blast occurred.

Her eight o'clock tea break had just ended and Taeko had put on her earphones and speaker to resume her shift on the second floor of the telephone exchange building. She saw the *pika* but heard no sound. (Only people far away from the hypocenter would report hearing the thunderous *don,* or "boom." Thus they referred to the atomic bombing as the *pikadon,* or "flash-boom," whereas those closer in, like Taeko, spoke simply of the *pika.*) Immediately Taeko was knocked down and buried underneath telephone equipment. Stunned, she freed herself and crawled to the stairwell, but it was clogged with the bodies of her coworkers.

Taeko looked out the second-floor window frame, now devoid of its glass. All of Hiroshima seemed to be on fire. In fact, within a few seconds of the explosion, fires had broken out in nearly every section of the city. Close to the hypocenter, the incredibly hot temperatures were sufficient to spontaneously ignite anything that could burn. Farther out, the shock waves dispersed kitchen fires and knocked down utility poles, snapping live wires. In a city constructed mostly of wood and paper, fuel for the inferno was abundant. Thousands of individual fires grew and merged, creating a vast conflagration that would completely burn everything combustible within a radius of about a mile and a quarter from the hypocenter. Those who were trapped alive beneath the debris that had once been their houses and schools and workplaces, along with those too injured by the blast to move, were burned alive.

Not wanting to suffer that fate, Taeko Teramae scanned the horrific scene for a refuge from the fire. Eventually she noticed that Hijiyama Hill, far to the east, seemed untouched. To get there, though, she would have to cross the Kyobashi River. Perhaps, she thought, the Tsurumi Bridge remained intact.

In any event, she realized that to have a chance, she had to get moving. Taeko jumped out the second-floor window and landed in the street.

Then she witnessed a ghastly sight. A seemingly endless procession was wending its way through the rubble-strewn streets. Many of the figures in this procession looked more like ghouls from some horror movie than they did human beings. Their faces were swollen grotesquely, their skin hung in tattered strips, and they shuffled along silently with elbows out and arms extended in front. Many survivors of the Hiroshima bombing would report having witnessed similar scenes. The severely burned had quickly discovered that shuffling along in this manner helped keep their burnt skin from rubbing, which was excruciating.

Unlike the victims she encountered in the street, Taeko could still run. Feeling no pain, she took off in the direction of the Tsurumi Bridge.

Sometime around 11 A.M., she reached the bridge. While the span had survived the blast, fires blocked its entrance. Taeko made her way to the seawall along the river, where she ran into a teacher she knew. The teacher seemed horrified at the condition of Taeko's face and left eye, but Taeko herself felt no pain.

With no way to cross the Tsurumi Bridge, Taeko had to make a decision. Either she could stay put and risk death by fire, or she could attempt to swim the river and risk death by drowning. The teacher convinced her that swimming was a better option. Together they jumped into the water.

After swimming for a while, Taeko grew tired and began floundering. "Take courage, child! You can't die here!" the teacher cried, grabbing her arm and pulling her along. Finally, they reached the other side. But the teacher decided to swim back to see whether she could

The intense heat from the atomic explosion, which raised surface temperatures within a mile of the hypocenter to more than 1,000°F, melted bottles and ceramic bowls into misshapen masses.

help anyone else. Taeko never again saw the woman who had saved her life.

Although the Kyobashi River now stood between her and the fires, Taeko continued moving. On the road up Hijiyama Hill, she passed fewer dead and wounded than she had seen on the other side of the river. Still, bodies lined the roadside.

By the early afternoon, now about halfway up the hill, Taeko reached an emergency aid station staffed by soldiers and nurses. By this time her face had begun to hurt quite a bit and she could barely see because of the swelling. She sat down at the end of the long line of people waiting to be treated. Many cried out in vain for water. Others begged to be killed.

Taeko waited a long time before her turn to be treated finally arrived. She could no longer see anything, so after they stitched her many cuts, the soldiers wrapped her head completely in a bandage, leaving a hole only for her nose and mouth.

Some of the soldiers who treated Taeko Teramae may have been sent up Hijiyama Hill hours earlier by Sakae Ito. Mrs. Ito's firebreak team had been assigned to clear a row of houses near the base of the hill. They were luckier than most Hiroshimans creating firebreaks on August 6, including the 8,000 junior high students. Most of those teenagers were working in the central city area and didn't survive the blast. On suburban Hijiyama Hill, Mrs. Ito's team was more than a mile from the hypocenter.

Even at that distance, however, the intense heat generated by Little Boy could still burn skin and ignite clothing. Just before she and her team were about to start tearing down the houses, Mrs. Ito's right shoulder suddenly caught fire. But she had no time to consider the cause of this bizarre phenomenon, for just as suddenly everything went dark. The shock wave had knocked her down and demolished the houses, burying her under the rubble.

Mrs. Ito scratched her way out and began helping to free her companions. Many of their faces were severely burned. Several could no longer see.

Soon a stream of horribly wounded people began flowing across the Tsurumi Bridge. Mrs. Ito recognized that the wounded had to keep moving forward or the bridge would become blocked. She spotted several soldiers who didn't seem severely injured and instructed them to lead the wounded up Hijiyama Hill. Then she went back to digging her comrades out of the rubble.

Reverend Kiyoshi Tanimoto had not had any trouble digging himself out of rubble. In Koi, at the far western reaches of Hiroshima, he had been twice as far from the hypocenter as Sakae Ito. In fact, after seeing the *pika*—

which from his vantage point resembled a sheet of sun sweeping from east to west—he'd had time to react before the shock wave hit. He dropped down between two large rocks in the garden of his wealthy acquaintance. Then roof tiles and pieces of wood rained down on him. Getting up, he saw that the house of his wealthy acquaintance had been demolished. A thick pall of smoke and dust hung over Koi, making the early morning seem more like twilight.

Like almost everyone in Hiroshima that day, Mr. Tanimoto assumed that a large conventional bomb had hit very close to where he was. After a while, however, he climbed atop a small hill to survey the scene. What he saw astonished him. A thick cloud blanketed the entire city.

Mr. Tanimoto became frightened for his wife and year-old daughter. He ran toward the burning city to find his family.

Not surprisingly, Mr. Tanimoto seemed to be the only person headed toward the center of the inferno. As he passed streams of burned and maimed victims, and as he saw acres upon acres of flattened houses, he began to comprehend the scope of the disaster. Moving east, he crossed the Yamate River. Finding his way blocked by fire, he followed the river northward. He intended to turn east again—toward the central city and the parsonage of his Nagarekawa United Church—once he reached the northern limit of the blaze.

Seeing no break in the inferno, however, he headed farther north toward Yokogawa Station. There he planned to pick up the tracks of the rail line that skirted northern Hiroshima in a semicircle. The arc of the rail line, he believed, would take him around the fire. A train burning on the tracks convinced Mr. Tanimoto that he had to go even farther north before he could safely get around the inferno. He ran two more miles to Gion, a suburb nestled in the northern foothills, before swim-ming across the Ota River. Altogether he had covered some seven miles, and he was still no closer to his church—or, he thought, to his wife and daughter.

Near the banks of the river, however, something miraculous happened: Mr. Tanimoto ran into his wife, who was carrying their daughter. Mrs. Tanimoto recounted how she had been buried beneath the wreckage of the parsonage, with the baby in her arms. Light shone through a tiny hole, and by clawing at that hole for a long time she managed to enlarge it enough to push the baby through. Then she climbed out herself. She and the baby were now headed north to the suburb of Ushida, where they would stay at a friend's house. Mr. Tanimoto still wanted to get back home because he believed he should help his congregation and the members of the neighbor-hood association. So he and his wife parted there.

The minister hadn't gone very far when he arrived at the East Parade Ground, where army recruits normally drilled. Now the field was littered with bomb victims too injured or weak to move. Many cried out for water.

On a nearby street Mr. Tanimoto found a basin and a water tap that still worked. He filled the basin and returned to the East Parade Ground. After he had given water to about 30 people, the minister realized that he couldn't help all the victims there. He had to make his way home to see to the needs of his church members and neighbors. "Excuse me," he said to victims who reached out and implored him to give them water. "I have many people to take care of." Then, basin in hand, he ran to the river and jumped down onto a spit of sand.

But he couldn't escape the pleas of the suffering. Hundreds of people lay stricken on the stretch of sand, and Mr. Tanimoto filled his basin in the river and brought them water.

A few small boats had been taking victims across the river. When one of these boats passed next to the spit, Mr. Tanimoto once again begged the pardon of the prostrate victims and jumped into it. The boat went to Asano Park, a private estate along the banks of the river. Among the throngs of injured people who had taken refuge in the wooded area the minister found several he knew. Nevertheless, he believed it his duty to render assistance in his own neighborhood, so he made another foray toward the central city area. The fires, still raging, forced him back.

Even though he couldn't do anything for the members of his neighborhood association or his congregation,

This photo, taken around 11 A.M. on August 6, shows victims at the Miyuki Bridge, 1.4 miles from the hypocenter.

the minister worked tirelessly to help victims in and around Asano Park. He found a boat and ferried the wounded across the river away from advancing fires. When fire reached Asano Park and threatened the refugees there, he organized the less severely injured men into a firefighting brigade. After two hours they managed to quell the blaze using buckets and basins full of water from one of the park's ponds. In the late afternoon he and a Jesuit priest ventured into the heart of the city after the fires there had finally begun to burn themselves out. Their mission was to find food for the people in Asano Park, and they succeeded, bringing back enough rice to feed about 100 victims. When nightfall arrived, Mr. Tanimoto plied the river in his boat, moving about 20 victims from a sandspit to higher ground ahead of the rising tide.

After a short, troubled sleep, the minister resumed his work as August 7 dawned. For five more days, in fact, Mr. Tanimoto would tend to the needs of the atomic bomb victims in Asano Park. He even traveled to Ushida, where his wife and daughter were staying, and brought back a tent to shelter some of the victims who were too critically injured to move.

All the while the Reverend Mr. Tanimoto was tending to the wounded in Asano Park, Communications Hospital director Michihiko Hachiya wished he could do the same in his institution. Unfortunately Dr. Hachiya had been seriously injured in the blast. Only by summoning all his willpower had he managed to traverse, in an eerie darkness, the several hundred yards from his ruined house to the gates of the Communications Bureau. There, adjacent to the hospital, friends put him on a stretcher and carried him inside to a makeshift emergency aid station. But fire soon swept through the Communications Bureau and the hospital, forcing the buildings to be

evacuated. As Dr. Hachiya faded in and out of conscious-
ness, his friends moved him from one small patch of
unburning ground to another.

"The sky was still dark," Dr. Hachiya observed when
he came to, "but whether it was evening or midday I
could not tell. It might even have been the next day. Time
had no meaning. What I had experienced might have
been crowded into a moment or been endured through
the monotony of eternity."

The cloud of dust and smoke had cleared enough to
give the doctor a horrifying view of his neighborhood as
well as the rest of the city:

> The streets were deserted except for the dead. Some
> looked as if they had been frozen by death while in the
> full action of flight; others lay sprawled as though some
> giant had flung them to their death from a great
> height.
>
>   Hiroshima was no longer a city, but a burnt-over
> prairie. To the east and to the west everything was flat-
> tened. The distant mountains seemed nearer than I
> could ever remember. . . . How small Hiroshima was
> with its houses gone.

An official assessment would later establish that 98
percent of the city's homes were destroyed by the blast
and fires unleashed by Little Boy.

Dr. Hachiya's spirits were boosted a bit by the arrival
of the Communications Hospital's chief of surgery, Dr.
Katsube. Everyone had assumed he was dead. Before
long, Dr. Katsube went to work on his colleague, sutur-
ing more than 40 wounds Dr. Hachiya had sustained. As
night fell, the director of the Communications Hospital
drifted off to sleep.

He awoke the following morning to a scene of chaos.
Though the exterior of the Communications Hospital

had withstood the atomic bomb, the blast had ripped through the windows like a hurricane. Broken window frames, glass fragments, and overturned and ruined medical equipment lay scattered everywhere. The interior walls were scarred and pitted by flying debris. And the fire had gutted the second floor.

The physical damage to the building exacerbated a more critical situation. Scores of severely burned and injured people had flocked to the Communications Hospital in search of shelter and treatment. They lined the floors of all the rooms, including the bathrooms, and spilled out into the corridors, which were all but impassable. Many victims had severe diarrhea and were vomiting, but they were too weak to move, so the filth accumulated everywhere. Dr. Hachiya thought of the many burn victims whose outer layers of skin had peeled away. They needed a sterile environment now to prevent infection, but instead they were living in the most unsanitary conditions imaginable.

Dr. Hachiya desperately wanted to bring order to the hospital and begin helping the victims, but with all the sutures he had received he couldn't move. The Communications Hospital had only a few nurses and doctors who were well enough to treat patients.

During the first days after the bombing, this situation was by no means unique. Of the 150 doctors who were practicing medicine in Hiroshima on August 5, all but about a dozen were killed or injured too severely the next day to work. Of the 1,750 nurses, 1,654 were killed or incapacitated. In the Red Cross Hospital, Hiroshima's best and largest, only one young doctor was well enough to treat the wounded. That man, Dr. Terufumi Sasaki, worked for three straight days with one hour's sleep as more than 10,000 victims poured into the Red Cross Hospital.

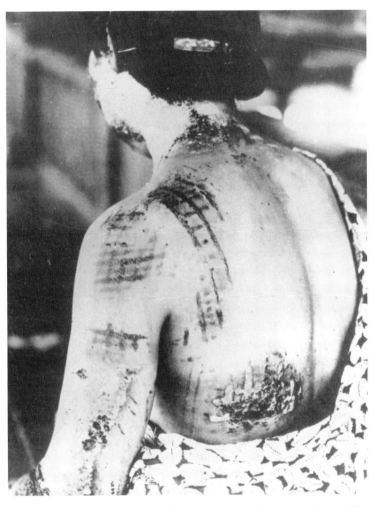

Because dark colors absorb heat and light colors reflect it, the burns on this victim's skin correspond to the pattern of her kimono. It wasn't just the heat that burned Hiroshimans' skin, however. Up to two miles from the hypo-center, the incredibly bright burst of light produced excruciating flash burns on exposed flesh.

The shortage of medical personnel made a horrific situation worse, but as army and private doctors trickled into the city from other areas of Japan, it became clear that no number of physicians would be sufficient to deal with the unfolding disaster. Up to 130,000 people had been injured, more than 43,000 of them severely. The sheer numbers of casualties, combined with a lack of shelter (let alone hospital space), shortages of medicine, and a total breakdown in sanitation, meant that a great number of people who had survived the blast and the fires were still going to die.

The appalling destruction Little Boy caused in Hiroshima was reproduced three days later at Nagasaki by an even more powerful plutonium implosion bomb. But casualties in Nagasaki were fewer, in part because the city's hills blocked much of the blast.

So many were dying at the Communications Hospital that Dr. Hachiya noted in his diary, "I had begun to accept death as a matter of course and ceased to respect its awfulness."

The able-bodied kept funeral pyres burning round the clock in a vain effort to keep ahead of the ever-accumulating number of corpses. Meanwhile, people wandered the destroyed city in search of the remains of their loved ones. In Japanese culture it is believed that a proper ceremony, including prompt and respectful cremation of the remains, is necessary for the souls of the dead to rest in peace. Unfortunately, many people would never find any trace of their loved ones to cremate.

As night fell on August 8, Dr. Hachiya—who had been moved to a room on the burned-out second floor of the Communications Hospital—looked out destroyed windows over the city. There was no electricity in

Hiroshima, but the light from cremation fires dotted the landscape as far as the eye could see. Closer to the hospital, he could see that the bomb's fury had not been totally extinguished after more than two days. "Concrete buildings near the center of the city, still afire on the inside, made eerie silhouettes against the night sky," Dr. Hachiya wrote.

The following day, though he was still unable to move about, Dr. Hachiya began to apply his scientific mind to a medical puzzle one of the Communications Hospital doctors had observed. Regardless of the type of injury they had sustained, nearly all the patients in the hospital displayed the same symptoms: loss of appetite, nausea, vomiting, and diarrhea, sometimes with blood in the stools. Other people, including some who had apparently not been injured at all, developed small hemorrhages under their skin. Such bloodspots are called petechiae. Neither Dr. Hachiya nor any of his colleagues had ever seen anything like this cluster of symptoms. Dr. Hachiya believed that a new type of weapon had been used on Hiroshima. The question was, what was it?

That night, as he waited in vain for sleep to come, Dr. Hachiya was haunted not so much by the unsolved medical mystery as by the suffering of a young orphaned girl in a nearby bed. "Mother, it hurts! I can't stand it," she called out repeatedly in the darkness.

The doctor had no way of knowing it, but there were a lot more Japanese orphans crying for their mothers that night. America had dropped its second atomic bomb, on the city of Nagasaki, earlier in the day.

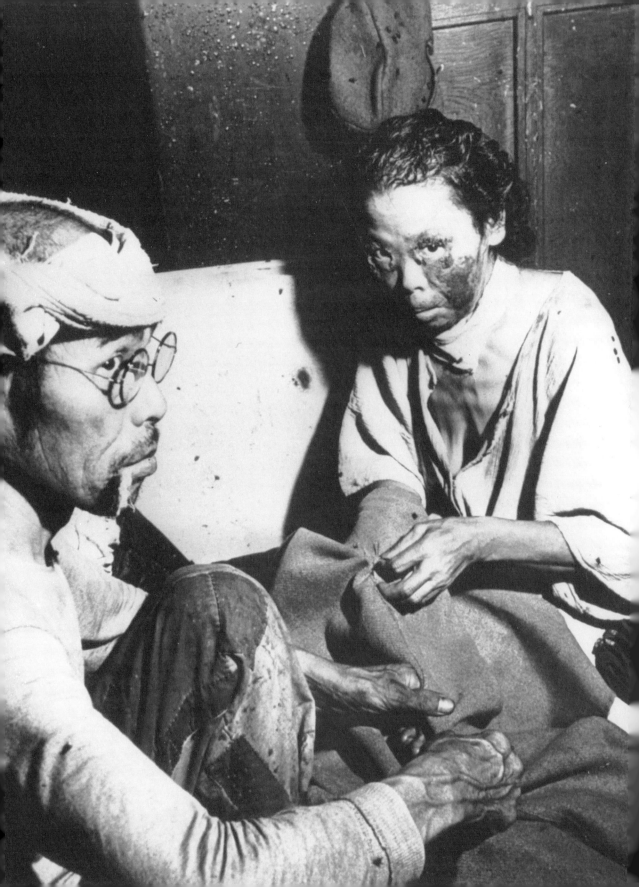

These survivors have taken up residence in a former bank building. The blast and fires of August 6 destroyed an estimated 98 percent of Hiroshima's houses. Shortages of food and medicine also plagued the city throughout the fall and winter following the atomic bombing. But there was another, less visible, reason survivors continued to fall ill and die.

Lingering Death 6

D r. Hachiya wasn't the only person wondering what sort of weapon had obliterated Hiroshima. A White House press release issued a few hours after the attack had announced that Little Boy was an atomic bomb, but Imperial leaders in Tokyo harbored doubts. Perhaps the American announcement was propaganda designed to frighten Japan into surrendering. Pending an investigation by Yoshio Nishina, the head of Japan's atomic bomb program, the Japanese leaders withheld news of Hiroshima's total destruction from their people. And the hard-liners in the cabinet refused to consider surrender, even though the American announcement had threatened Japan with "a rain of ruin from the air, the like of which has never been seen on this earth."

By August 9 the leaders in Tokyo had Nishina's preliminary

conclusions: that the Hiroshima bomb had indeed been atomic. Bad news had also arrived from Manchuria early in the morning. Despite its nonaggression treaty with Japan, the Soviet Union had declared war and launched an offensive against Japan's Kwantung Army. A war conference convened in emergency session to discuss how to proceed. Soon a messenger entered with a third piece of bad news: Nagasaki had been destroyed by another atomic bomb.

Prime Minister Kantaro Suzuki argued for acceptance of the Potsdam Declaration and immediate surrender. But the militarists still clung to the hope that their *Ketsu-Go* strategy could force the Americans to negotiate peace terms favorable to Japan. "With luck," maintained General Yoshijiro Umezu, chief of the Army General Staff, "we will be able to repulse the invaders before they land. I can say with confidence that we will be able to destroy the major part of an invading force." The conference broke up with no agreement on what to do next.

At a cabinet meeting later in the day, those in favor of surrender and those who wanted to fight to the death argued back and forth for hours. Finally, Prime Minister Suzuki announced the convening of an Imperial conference. Suzuki knew that Emperor Hirohito had decided to abandon tradition and intervene personally to stop the war if his cabinet couldn't reach a consensus.

Several hours of heated discussion made it clear that no consensus would be forthcoming. Foreign Minister Shigenori Togo, with agreement from Navy Minister Mitsumasa Yonai, urged that Japan accept the Potsdam Declaration with one stipulation: that the emperor's status be guaranteed. Ironically, this was exactly the counsel Togo had rejected less than three weeks before, when the diplomat Naotake Sato had told him that Japan could hope for no better surrender terms. Now a furious

General Korechika Anami shouted his objection. Unless Japan could dictate the terms of its surrender, the head of the General Staff sputtered, "we must continue fighting with courage and find life in death!"

To the amazement of most of those present, Prime Minister Suzuki asked the emperor to express his wishes. The ministers jumped to their feet and bowed their heads as the man-god rose to speak:

> I have given serious thought to the situation prevailing at home and abroad and have concluded that continuing the war can only mean destruction for the nation and prolongation of bloodshed and cruelty in the world. I cannot bear to see my innocent people suffer any longer. Ending the war is the only way to restore world peace and to relieve the nation from the terrible distress with which it is burdened. . . .
>
> It goes without saying that it is unbearable for me to see the brave and loyal fighting men of Japan disarmed. It is equally unbearable that others who have rendered me devoted service should now be punished as instigators of the war. Nevertheless, the time has come when we must bear the unbearable.

After the emperor left the room, his cabinet reluctantly agreed to accept his wishes.

On August 10 the Japanese Foreign Ministry notified the Allies, via the neutral countries of Sweden and Switzerland, of Japan's acceptance of the Potsdam Declaration—provided the emperor remained the nation's sovereign ruler. That same day, senior army officers were briefed on the decision.

Five more days would pass before the people of Hiroshima learned of the decision to surrender. During that time, conditions in the destroyed city scarcely improved. In the overcrowded hospital wards, in the

World War II officially ends as the Japanese foreign minister signs the instrument of surrender aboard the USS *Missouri,* September 22, 1945.

dank and dark basement of the gutted Fukuya department store, in makeshift open-air treatment centers where rows of victims were arranged—in the words of one witness—"like so many cod fish spread out for drying," people continued to suffer horribly and die.

Yet in the midst of their agony, many Hiroshimans remained hopeful that Japan might still prevail. In the absence of newspapers and radio, the only source of information became the outsiders who entered the city to look for relatives or help victims. Rumors abounded. One that swept through the Communications Hospital said that Japan had attacked the West Coast cities of the United States with the same kind of weapon that had destroyed Hiroshima. "The whole atmosphere of the ward changed," Dr. Hachiya recorded in his diary, "and for the first time since Hiroshima was bombed, everyone became cheerful and bright. Those who had been hurt the most were the happiest. Jokes were made, and some began singing the victory song. . . . Everyone was now convinced that the tide of the war had turned."

At noon on August 15, however, all hopes for victory were dashed. In a prerecorded message broadcast over Japanese radio, Emperor Hirohito announced the nation's surrender to his subjects. "[T]he enemy," he said, "has begun to employ a new and most cruel bomb, the power of which to do damage is indeed incalculable, taking the toll of many innocent lives."

In the city where that new and most cruel bomb had first been unleashed, the emperor's announcement came as a heavy blow. "The one word—surrender—had produced a greater shock than the bombing of our city," Dr. Hachiya wrote. The initial shock soon gave way to anger, then to despair. All the suffering, all the sorrow Hiroshima had endured would be in vain.

And the suffering continued. About five days after the bombing, the death rate had stabilized and had then slowly begun to decline. A week or so later, the death rate unexpectedly began to rise dramatically. Bloody stools, petechiae, sores in the mouth and throat, bleeding gums, and a new symptom—hair loss—appeared in many people who had seemed to be getting better. The majority of these people died, often in severe pain, from massive internal bleeding. When a few of Hiroshima's doctors began conducting autopsies—a practice discouraged by the Japanese authorities—they discovered changes in all the internal organs. The blood of victims also showed very low counts of white blood cells, which fight infection, and of platelets, which help blood coagulate. In fact, so low were victims' platelet counts that six or seven hours after death their blood still had not coagulated. Hiroshima's doctors were at a loss to explain what these symptoms meant.

In America a few people close to the atomic bomb program knew what the symptoms meant. They meant that the Manhattan Project scientists had grossly underestimated the bomb's radiation effects.

When Little Boy exploded, the blast, the heat, and the visible light weren't the only forms of energy released. Massive amounts of radiation—such as X rays and gamma rays, neutrons, and beta particles—invisible to the eye but harmful to the body in large doses, had also propagated outward in all directions. The radiation, capable of traveling through skin, destroyed cells and penetrated the internal organs of people who were exposed. Those who had received the highest radiation doses—those closest to the hypocenter—had died within a few hours or days. Understandably, severe burns and other injuries had masked the radiation effects in most of these victims. Those exposed to lesser but still dangerously high amounts of radiation, many of whom appeared to be well, had actually sustained internal damage. The radiation they had absorbed destroyed their capacity to make new blood cells, which a healthy body must do continually because blood cells live for only a few weeks. When that interval had elapsed and there were no new cells to replace dead ones, the victims became ill.

On September 3, Hiroshima's doctors finally found out why bomb victims were still dying a month after Little Boy fell on their city. In the burned-out ruins of a bank, Dr. Masao Tsuzuki, a professor at Tokyo Imperial University, gave a presentation on radiation effects. During the 1920s, while he was a graduate student at the University of Pennsylvania, Professor Tsuzuki had exposed rabbits to massive amounts of radiation. He discovered that the radiation produced lingering—and lethal—effects in the rabbits. What the human beings who were now suffering from radiation sickness needed, the 65-year-old professor told his audience of Hiroshima doctors, was total rest, a nutritious diet, calcium and liver injections, and blood transfusions. Only the first of these suggestions was even the slightest bit practical in a city that had been reduced to ruins and faced extreme shortages of food and medical supplies.

Reports of radiation sickness among the Hiroshima survivors had begun to trickle back to the United States. Journalists had even picked up a rumor that Hiroshima would be unsafe for human habitation for the next 75 years because of high levels of residual radioactivity in the soil.

General Leslie Groves was troubled by these reports. Groves viewed the Manhattan Project as his crowning achievement, and now questions about the use of radiation as a weapon were threatening to taint his legacy. It wasn't supposed to have been that way. The scientists had viewed the bomb as a blast weapon. The only people who would be exposed to potentially deadly levels of radiation would already be dead from the blast, they believed. Clearly, though, something was amiss in Hiroshima.

To get ahead of the negative publicity, Groves dispatched his right-hand man, General Thomas Farrell, to Hiroshima with 15 tons of medical supplies and a team of scientists. To everyone's relief, a hasty examination

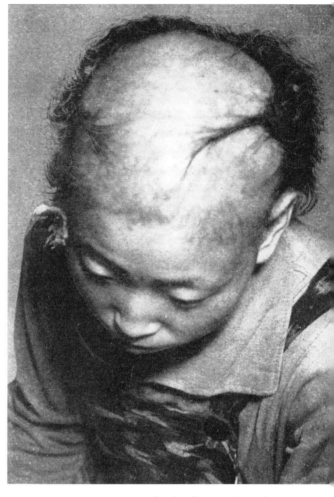

In the days and weeks after the atomic bombing, Hiroshima residents—including many who like this young girl had apparently escaped serious injury—began losing their hair. The cause: radiation sickness, which would claim thousands of lives long after the war had ended.

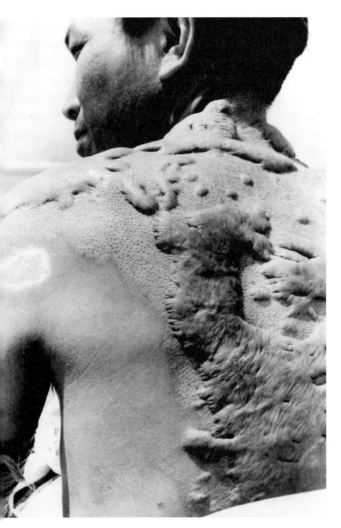

Keloids, masses of thick scar tissue produced by flash and thermal burns, disfigured survivors of the atomic bombing.

revealed no evidence of abnormal levels of radioactivity in the soil. Hiroshima was *not* uninhabitable. And, it would seem, people who had not yet gotten sick had nothing to fear from lingering radioactivity. What the scientists failed to consider, however, was that high levels of radioactivity could linger in the body's tissues and organs.

Groves himself moved to defend the bomb at a Senate hearing in November. When a senator asked what happened to a typical radiation victim, the general replied, "He can have enough [radiation] so that he will be killed instantly. He can have a smaller amount which will cause him to die rather soon, as I understand it from the doctors, without undue suffering. In fact, they say it is a very pleasant way to die." That was an outrageous lie, as anyone would know who visited the hospitals of Hiroshima, where radiation victims, suffering from symptoms that included fever, nausea, severe abdominal distress, pain upon swallowing, and massive hemorrhaging, lingered at death's door for days or weeks before succumbing.

Groves's chief medical officer, Stafford Warren, also downplayed the radiation effects of the atomic bomb in the Senate hearing. Warren reported that deaths attributable to radiation constituted no more than 7 or 8 percent of the total killed in Hiroshima. A more thorough study conducted the following year by the United States Strategic Bombing Survey found that the actual numbers were at least twice that high and maybe even reached 20 percent. An equal number of people, the study concluded, had sustained radiation injuries but survived.

But that also did not represent the full story. As the years passed, survivors of the Hiroshima bombing—called *hibakusha* in Japan—suffered much higher than normal rates of various types of cancer. Among *hibakusha* nearest to the hypocenter, for example, leukemia struck at an estimated 10 to 50 times the expected rate. Cancers of the lungs, thyroid, stomach, liver, breast, salivary glands, and urinary tract also occurred in abnormally high numbers. The weapon dropped on Hiroshima to end the war continued to kill long after the war had ended.

Hibakusha who were fortunate enough to avoid cancer bore other physical reminders of their ordeal. Keloids—thick deposits of scar tissue that looked as if they had been made by the claws of a wild animal—disfigured the skin of burn victims. Cataracts, which normally affect only older people, clouded the eyes of children and adults alike. Some children experienced stunted growth. Others who had been in their mothers' wombs at the time of the bombing were born with abnormally small heads and a form of mental retardation.

Of course, the long-term effects of the bomb weren't foremost in the minds of the *hibakusha* who scratched out a precarious existence through the fall and winter of 1945–46. Food was scarce; many survived on dumplings of horseweed grass and ground acorns. Water shortages were chronic. Hovels constructed from the rubble couldn't keep out the winter cold. Lawlessness abounded. And, to add to the misery, a typhoon struck just as the city was beginning to come to life again. High winds knocked down makeshift shelters, and torrential rains turned acres of the bombed-out wasteland into lakes, drowning many people, including teams of doctors who had come from Kyoto to aid the atomic bomb victims.

Throughout that first fall and winter, the author Peter Wyden has written, the "world acted as if nothing special had occurred in Hiroshima." Neither the Japanese

A THOUSAND PAPER CRANES

Twelve-year-old Sadako Sasaki, a student at Nobori-cho Junior High School, seemed to be in perfect health. The friendly, popular Sadako loved to run, and she was faster than anyone else in her class. But after she suffered a fainting spell in the school yard, doctors discovered that she had leukemia. On August 6,

1945, Sadako, then two years old, had been about a mile from the hypocenter of the atomic bomb.

In Japan, origami—the art of folding paper into three-dimensional figures—is a popular pastime, and a Japanese folk belief says that a person who folds 1,000 paper cranes will be cured of any illness. From her bed at the Hiroshima Red Cross Hospital, Sadako folded paper cranes each day, hoping to reach 1,000 and be restored to health. She didn't make it. On October 25, 1955, Sadako died.

To commemorate their friend's life and express their desire for peace, Sadako's classmates spearheaded an effort to raise money for a monument. Today paper cranes from around the world adorn the Children's Peace Monument in Hiroshima.

The Children's Peace Monument.

government nor the American occupation authorities extended any extraordinary assistance. Perhaps this was because Curtis LeMay's B-29s had laid waste to so many Japanese cities, and the entire country needed rebuilding. Perhaps also there was a reluctance to look too closely at what had happened—at what was still happening—in the city where the concept of total war had been carried to its horrifying though logical conclusion.

"Mr. President, I have blood on my hands," J. Robert Oppenheimer would tell Harry Truman. In a sense, it was a statement that applied to all of America—and one that neither Truman nor the rest of the country wanted to hear. Nor would the United States, victorious in a "good war" against a ruthless enemy, want to ponder the judgment of Admiral William Leahy, Truman's chief military adviser, on the means used to end that war: "[W]e had adopted an ethical standard common to the barbarians of the Dark Ages."

For a time, the Japanese too seemed to want to forget—to forget how they had enthusiastically followed the militarists who ignited the Pacific war; to forget how they had pursued the war with singular brutality; to forget how their leaders' *Ketsu-Go* strategy had arguably made the tragedy of Hiroshima inevitable; indeed, to forget the *hibakusha* themselves, who for years were discriminated against and shunned.

With the passage of time Japan, the United States, and the world would begin to come to terms with what happened in Hiroshima. Whether or not use of the bomb was necessary from a military standpoint or justifiable from a moral one, whether or not it ultimately saved lives, the hell unleashed by this single bomb staggers the imagination. The precise number of Hiroshimans killed will never be known, but estimates range up to 140,000 by the end of 1945, and 200,000 by 1950.

The Cenotaph for the A-bomb Victims, dedicated on August 6, 1952, was the first monument in Hiroshima's Peace Memorial Park. The stone chest under the arch houses a register of the names of all Hiroshima's deceased atomic bomb victims.

"An Exhibit for Peace"

E ven before Manhattan Project scientists had figured out how to create an atomic bomb, Edward Teller dreamed of an even more destructive weapon. The Hungarian-born physicist had been assigned to Los Alamos, but he contributed little to the effort that culminated in the Hiroshima and Nagasaki bombs. Instead, he spent his time pursuing theories and calculations that might someday make the doomsday weapon he called "the Super" a reality.

The atomic bomb unleashed its enormous power through nuclear fission—by splitting the nuclei of the very heavy elements uranium and plutonium. Teller's Super, on the other hand, would fuse the nuclei of the lightest element, hydrogen, transforming it into helium. The energy thereby released would make the fission bomb seem tiny by comparison:

nuclear fusion is what gives the sun and stars their energy; it is the force that powers the universe.

Teller's early designs all proved unworkable, however, and his Super remained just a dream until after the war. Then mathematician Stanislaw Ulam provided a critical insight: the hydrogen bomb could be a two-stage device, with the first stage consisting of an atomic bomb detonation. Teller realized that in the second stage, X rays produced by the atomic explosion could trigger the burning of liquid deuterium, a heavy form of hydrogen. If temperatures were high enough in this thermonuclear device, hydrogen nuclei would fuse.

On August 6, 1952, Hiroshima dedicated the first of what would be many monuments in the city's Peace Memorial Park, which is situated on the delta island between the Honkawa and Motoyasu Rivers. The Cenotaph for the A-bomb Victims—officially called the Memorial Monument for Hiroshima, City of Peace—was an arch that rose over a stone chest. That chest housed a register of the names of all Hiroshima's deceased atomic bomb victims. An inscription on the side read: "Let all the souls here rest in peace; for we shall not repeat the evil."

Less than three months after the unveiling of Hiroshima's first monument to peace, the United States unveiled a new instrument of war. On the small Pacific island of Elugelab, American scientists successfully detonated the world's first hydrogen bomb, dubbed Mike. Its fireball swelled to a diameter of more than three miles, leaving a 200-foot-deep, mile-wide crater where the island had been. Hiroshima had been destroyed by a bomb that yielded the equivalent of about 12.5 kilotons—12,500 tons—of TNT. Mike exploded with a force equivalent to about 10.4 megatons—more than 10 *million* tons—of dynamite. Now America had in its possession a weapon almost 1,000 times as destructive as the one unleashed on Hiroshima.

By this time, however, the United States no longer had a monopoly on nuclear weapons. In 1949 the Soviet Union had successfully detonated its first atomic bomb. Within a year of the Mike test, the USSR would also have a thermonuclear bomb.

Over the years, other nations would follow the two founding members into the nuclear "club": England, France, China, South Africa (which later became the only country ever to voluntarily give up its nuclear arsenal), India, Pakistan, probably Israel. While a conflict involving any of these nations could theoretically have led to Hiroshima-like catastrophes, the most acute danger of nuclear war always seemed to lie with the United States and the USSR.

The period between the end of World War II and the early 1990s became known as the Cold War era. During this time, a tense standoff between the United States and the Soviet Union, the world's most powerful nations, dominated international affairs. Combined, the two countries—bitter ideological enemies—plunged trillions of dollars into developing and producing weapons with which to destroy each other. In addition to more—and more powerful—thermonuclear warheads, each side developed intercontinental ballistic missiles (ICBMs) capable of rapidly delivering those terrible weapons to enemy cities. Smaller, more efficient warhead designs and improved targeting systems meant that a single missile could deliver multiple warheads to different targets. Within a half hour of its launch, one of America's Minuteman III ICBMs could unleash, anywhere in the USSR, almost 85 times the destruction produced by the Little Boy atomic bomb that obliterated Hiroshima.

What had evolved was a balance of terror: the United

Each year on August 6, Hiroshimans place paper lanterns in the Motoyasu River to commemorate their loved ones killed by the atomic bombing. In the background is the former Industrial Promotion Hall. Now called the A-bomb Dome, it serves as a monument in Peace Memorial Park.

States and the Soviet Union menaced each other with the threat of annihilation. Despite more than four decades of Cold War conflict, however, the two nations never went to war directly with each other. They didn't dare. A war between the superpowers could have escalated into a nuclear confrontation. Having seen what that meant in Hiroshima, with one comparatively small atomic weapon, leaders on both sides shrank from the possibility of an even more cataclysmic disaster. As McGeorge Bundy, who had served as national security adviser to President John F. Kennedy, noted in a 1969 article,

> In light of the certain prospect of retaliation, there has been literally no chance at all that any sane political authority, in either the United States or the Soviet Union, would consciously choose to start a nuclear war. . . . [A] decision that would bring even one hydrogen bomb on one city of one's own country would be recognized in advance as a catastrophic blunder; ten bombs on ten cities would be a disaster beyond history; and a hundred bombs on a hundred cities are unthinkable."

Indeed, 100 hydrogen bombs on 100 cities might be more than enough to destroy the entire human race. At least, that's what a group of prominent scientists concluded in the mid-1980s. Massive fires triggered by the hydrogen bombs would release huge amounts of smoke and soot into the atmosphere, which would block the sun's rays, these scientists declared. The surface of the earth would remain in semidarkness for an extended period. Temperatures would plummet, and the planet would be plunged into what the scientists referred to as a "nuclear winter." After plant life died out, the animals higher up on the food chain would soon follow. Eventually the human survivors of the nuclear war—both in the countries that had fought the war and in the countries that weren't involved—would have nothing to eat. The extinction of the human race might well ensue—a possibility that would presumably deter even the most reckless and fanatical of leaders.

Perhaps Alfred Nobel's tormented dream of a weapon so horrible that it would make war obsolete has finally been fulfilled, at least in part. It's true that nations and peoples are still taking up arms against one another with depressing regularity. But leaders seem to have recognized that the kind of pitiless, no-holds-barred conflict that prevailed in World War II—total war—is no longer an option.

While recognizing that much progress remains to be made, many Hiroshimans would no doubt be heartened by this development. In their search for meaning in the tragedy of August 6, 1945, *hibakusha* often expressed the hope that their suffering might bear witness to the evils of war and inspire others to choose peace.

The city of Hiroshima itself has adopted the mission of fostering peace. As it slowly rose from the ashes and rubble after the war, Hiroshima incorporated among its gleaming skyscrapers and prosperous business districts a host of monuments and memorials, reminders to the world that the *ayamachi*—the mistake—must never be repeated. More than 70 of these monuments and memorials lie in and around the serenely beautiful Peace Memorial Park. The Peace Museum, which houses artifacts from the bombing along with the artwork and personal recollections of survivors, receives more than a million visitors, from all parts of the world, each year.

But physical monuments and museums constitute only a small part of Hiroshima's efforts for peace. Programs such as a summer school for children and seminars and conferences for adults encourage people of all ages to think about what they can do to promote peace.

And each year, on August 6, the city of Hiroshima marks the anniversary of the bombing. At 8:15 A.M., tens of thousands of people gather in Peace Memorial Park, ground that on that long-ago August morning witnessed some of war's most unspeakable horrors. The names of all the *hibakusha* who died during the previous year are added to the Cenotaph for the A-bomb Victims. The mayor delivers the annual peace declaration, which typically touches on current conflicts and threats to peace, especially nuclear proliferation. At dusk Hiroshimans gather along the banks of the city's rivers with paper lanterns, the sides of which may bear the names of relatives who died as a result of the atomic bombing. After the candles are lit, the lanterns are placed on the water, a symbol of life. Through this simple ceremony, it is hoped, the souls of the dead will find peace.

But the thousands of tiny beacons drifting downriver to the Inland Sea are more than just an offering to the souls of the victims. They represent a hope, a prayer, a reminder, and a warning—the gift of a devastated city and its citizens to all of humanity.

Shinzo Hamai, a *hibakusha* and longtime mayor of the city, put it succinctly. "The people of Hiroshima," he said, "ask nothing of the world except that we be allowed to offer ourselves as an exhibit for peace."

Perhaps one day all the world's people might finally acknowledge—and honor—that exhibit.

Chronology

1931   Japan's Kwantung Army initiates the conquest of Manchuria

1937   Japanese and Chinese soldiers fight a minor skirmish near Peking on July 7, and Japan uses the incident to justify conquering all of China; American president Franklin Roosevelt calls for international action to "quarantine the [Japanese] aggressors"

1939   United States announces that it will terminate its trade agreement with Japan to protest continued Japanese aggression in China; Nazi Germany invades Poland on September 1; on September 3 England and France declare war on Germany, touching off World War II

1940   United States imposes economic sanctions on Japan; German spring offensive leads to the rapid conquest of Denmark, Norway, the Netherlands, Belgium, and Luxembourg; Fascist Italy declares war on England and France on June 10; France falls on June 22; Japan, Germany, and Italy sign Tripartite Pact, creating the Axis alliance, in September

1941   Japan and the Soviet Union sign five-year neutrality treaty in April; in June, Germany invades USSR; in July, Japan occupies French colony of Indochina, and United States responds by freezing all Japanese assets in America and imposing an oil embargo; at a September 6 Imperial conference, Japanese leaders decide to launch a surprise attack on the U.S. Pacific Fleet at Pearl Harbor, Hawaii, unless a negotiated settlement to the two nations' differences is obtained; on December 7, Japanese planes attack Pearl Harbor, sinking 18 ships and killing more than 2,400 American servicemen; the following day, Congress declares war on Japan; Germany and Italy declare war on the United States on December 11; on December 22, Japanese troops land on the main Philippine island, Luzon, soon forcing American and Filipino soldiers to retreat to the Bataan Peninsula

1942   Bataan contingent surrenders to Japanese on April 9; Corregidor surrenders on May 6; Bataan Death March ensues; Americans win decisive naval battle of Midway in June; United States, in conjunction with Great Britain and Canada, begins work on producing an atomic bomb; the effort, code-named the Manhattan Project, is headed by

General Leslie R. Groves and the physicist J. Robert Oppenheimer; U.S. Marines begin landing on Guadalcanal in the Solomon Islands on August 7

1943 From the Casablanca Conference in January, President Franklin Roosevelt announces that the Allies will insist on unconditional surrender from Germany and Japan; fighting on Guadalcanal finally ends on February 9

1944 During battle for island of Saipan (June 15 to July 9), Americans suffer 14,000 casualties, while nearly 30,000 Japanese soldiers fight to the death and many Japanese civilians commit suicide; in October, during the Battle of Leyte Gulf, Japanese deploy kamikaze, or suicide, pilots; on November 14, Marianas-based B-29s make their first air raid on Tokyo

1945 Curtis LeMay assumes command of 21st Bomber Command in January, initiates incendiary bombing attacks on Japanese cities; month-long battle for island of Iwo Jima (February 16 to March 16) costs 25,000 American casualties, including 6,800 dead; March 9–10 firebomb raid on Tokyo kills up to 100,000, injures 1 million, and leaves 1 million homeless; on April 1, American troops land on Okinawa, where bitter fighting will last until late June; on April 12, Franklin Roosevelt dies, and Harry Truman becomes president; Germany surrenders in May; on July 16, United States successfully tests atomic bomb near Alamogordo, New Mexico; on July 26, the Potsdam Declaration reiterates the Allies' demand that Japan surrender unconditionally, but Japan does not respond; on August 6, the United States drops an atomic bomb on Hiroshima, destroying the city and killing an estimated 140,000 Japanese by the end of 1945; a second atomic bomb is dropped on Nagasaki on August 9, the same day the USSR launches an offensive against Japanese troops in Manchuria; on August 10, Japan notifies Allies of its acceptance of the Potsdam Declaration; Japan officially surrenders on September 22

Bibliography

A-Bomb: A City Tells Its Story. Hiroshima, Japan: Hiroshima Peace Culture Foundation, 1972.

Frank, Richard B. *Downfall: The End of the Imperial Japanese Empire.* New York: Random House, 1999.

Hachiya, Michihiko, M.D. *Hiroshima Diary.* Tr. and ed. by Warner Wells, M.D. Chapel Hill: The University of North Carolina Press, 1995.

Hersey, John. *Hiroshima,* rev. ed. New York: Vintage Books, 1989.

Kennedy, David M. "Victory at Sea." *Atlantic Monthly* (March 1999): 51–76.

McCullough, David. *Truman.* New York: Simon & Schuster, 1992.

Rhodes, Richard. *Dark Sun: The Making of the Hydrogen Bomb.* New York: Simon & Schuster, 1995.

———. *The Making of the Atomic Bomb.* New York: Simon & Schuster, 1987.

The Spirit of Hiroshima. Hiroshima, Japan: Hiroshima Peace Memorial Museum, 1999.

Wyden, Peter. *Day One: Before Hiroshima and After.* New York: Simon & Schuster, 1984.

Websites

A-Bomb WWW Museum
www.csi.ad.jp/ABOMB

Hiroshima Archive
www.lclark.edu/~history/HIROSHIMA

Voice of Hibakusha
www.inicom.com/hibakusha/

Index

Index

JOHN ZIFF is a senior editor at Chelsea House. He lives near Philadelphia with his wife, Clare, and children, Jane and Peter.

JILL McCAFFREY has served for four years as national chairman of the Armed Forces Emergency Services of the American Red Cross. Ms. McCaffrey also serves on the board of directors for Knollwood—the Army Distaff Hall. The former Jill Ann Faulkner, a Massachusetts native, is the wife of Barry R. McCaffrey, a member of President Bill Clinton's cabinet and director of the White House Office of National Drug Control Policy. The McCaffreys are the parents of three grown children: Sean, a major in the U.S. Army; Tara, an intensive care nurse and captain in the National Guard; and Amy, a seventh grade teacher. The McCaffreys also have two grandchildren, Michael and Jack.

Picture Credits